To
Make a
Prairie

Poets on Poetry

Donald Hall, General Editor

To
Make a
Prairie

Essays on Poets, Poetry,
and Country Living

MAXINE KUMIN

Ann Arbor   The University of Michigan Press

1983   1982   1981   5   4   3

Library of Congress Cataloging in Publication Data
Kumin, Maxine W
   To Make a prairie.

   (Poets on Poetry)
   1. Kumin, Maxine W.—Interviews.   2. Poetry—
Addresses, essays, lectures.   I. Title.
II. Series.
PS3521.U638Z475   808.1   79-13289
ISBN 0-472-06306-5

Acknowledgments

Grateful acknowledgment is made to the following publishers for permission to reprint copyrighted materials:

Doubleday & Company Inc. for "The Muse" by Barry Spacks from *The Company of Children*. Copyright © 1969 by Barry Spacks. Reprinted by permission of Doubleday & Company Inc.

Harper & Row, Publishers, Inc. for excerpts and complete poems by Maxine Kumin from *The Privilege*, copyright © 1965 by Maxine Kumin, *The Nightmare Factory*, copyright © 1970 by Maxine Kumin, and *Up Country*, copyright © 1972 by Maxine Kumin.

Indiana University Press for "Award" by Ray Durem from *New Negro Poets: USA*, edited by Langston Hughes.

Little, Brown and Company in association with the Atlantic Monthly Press for "The Even Sea" by May Swenson from *New and Selected Things Taking Place*. Copyright 1954, © 1958, 1978 by May Swenson.

Viking Penguin Inc. for excerpts and complete poems by Maxine Kumin from *House Bridge Fountain Gate* and *The Retrieval System*.

To make a prairie it takes a clover and one bee,
One clover, and a bee,
and revery.
The revery alone will do,
If bees be few.
Emily Dickinson, Poem 1755

Contents

I
Interviews

The following interviews, arranged chronologically and trimmed considerably, nevertheless overlap in places. I have let certain repetitions stand where they seemed necessary as connective tissue. The Interlochen interview was conducted by a group of high school students, all of them would-be writers; I tried to make my own experiences with the creative process useful to them.

An Interview

With Virginia Elson and Beverlee Hughes

"The Dreamer, the Dream" is a special favorite of ours because it seems to us to be so perfectly what John Ciardi defines as a poem, "a way of meaning more than one thing at a time." Ciardi was actually referring to your "Morning Swim," and he added ". . . that poem is also, of course, about poetry. . . . " We wonder if you would care to discuss "The Dreamer, the Dream" from this point of view, for it seems to us that this poem, too, is "about poetry." [The poem appears in its entirety following Maxine Kumin's reply.]

"The Dreamer, the Dream" is, of course, about poetry as well as dreams and mushrooms. Somehow, all three come together in my head, for they are all to some degree unconscious, or at least secret, processes. It is absurdly anthropomorphic to speak of mushrooms as "unconscious," but to come upon them in the woods as I have so often done in fact, and in this instance in the poem, is to come upon a kind of revelation, an insight not unlike the insight that gives rise to a poem. These particular

---

Originally appeared in *Yes: A Magazine of Poetry* 4, no. 3 (Spring-Summer 1974). Reprinted by permission.

mushrooms are *armillaria mellea*. Country folk call them "honey mushrooms" because they are so sweet.

The Dreamer, The Dream

After the sleeper has burst his night pod
climbed up out of its silky holdings
the dream must stumble alone now
must mope in the hard eye of morning

in search of some phantom outcome
while on both sides of the tissue
the dreamer walks into the weather
past time in September woods in the rain

where the butternuts settle around him
louder than tears and in fact he comes
upon great clusters of honey mushrooms
breaking the heart of old oak

a hundred caps grotesquely piggyback
on one another, a caramel mountain
all powdered with their white spores
printing themselves in no notebook

and all this they do in secret
climbing behind his back
lumbering from their dark fissure
going up like a dream going on.

In the same essay ("The Art of Maxine Kumin," The Saturday Review, *March 25, 1972) Ciardi writes, "Maxine Kumin knows how to see things. She teaches me, by example, to use my own eyes. When she looks at something I have seen, she makes me see it better. When she looks at something I do not know, I therefore trust her." Have you always observed things with a "master eye," or have you trained yourself to see this way? If training has been involved, can you describe it? Do you see most objects in a double or multiple sense when you first observe them?*

I am embarrassed to think that I look at things with a "master eye," and certainly no conscious training has been involved. It's true that minutiae fascinate me and I am forever squirreling up the Latin names of things after I find out what they properly are. Naming things is a way of owning them, I guess. I do collect various mushroom books, for example, mostly to help an amateur with identifications and also for the beauty of the books themselves. It's much the same with books on wild edible plants, wild flowers, ferns, birds, and the rest. It seems important to have the facts, partly for accuracy and partly out of inquisitiveness. No, I don't think I see objects in a multiple way at all. I may be struck emotionally in a way separate from identification but I usually don't know this at the time.

Richard Moore, reviewing your second collection of poems, The Privilege, *wrote, "Maxine Kumin is an accomplished and professional poet of what might be called the Bishop-Lowell-Sexton school." How do you feel about this description? Do you think that such categorizing of poets by critics is a service or a disservice to the poet and to the reader?*

Categories scare me. I guess I think it is up to the critic to define the schools and up to the poet not to ponder these matters lest he/she begin to brood on them. I suspect that what Moore is saying is enormously flattering, and that puts me off. Lowell and Sexton have often been linked together as so-called confessional poets, which Miss Bishop assuredly is not. The three have in common, at least in the earlier works of Sexton and Lowell, a particularly brilliant craftsmanship. Also, all three are adept at telling a story. But you find me interpreting a question and I had said that I didn't think I ought to; so I'll put this one aside.

Would you care to mention those writers who have had, in your opinion, the greatest influence on your work? Have you ever felt restricted by them . . . experienced what Harold Bloom in The Anxiety of Influence *calls that haunting shadow of "prior visions of other poems" by other poets?*

Two writers were always important to me in terms of their poetics: Yeats and Auden. I was absolutely bowled over by Auden when I first read him during my undergraduate years. He has never palled for me. In all truth, I have not felt restricted by "prior visions of other poems"—some of this is a happy ignorance at least before the fact of poems which mine might resemble. There must be some unconscious deriving and rubbing off.

Diane Wakoski (in "The Craft of Carpenters, Plumbers, and Mechanics, American Poetry Review, *November-December, 1973) writes,*

> The poetry world is the only one I know where an amateur can get just as much attention as a serious professional. It is the one world where "new" and "talented" people get more attention than poets who have already proved their craft, and it is, oddly, a place where there seems to be no middle ground, either you are immortal, or you are no good.

Do you agree with her analysis?

There is no middle ground in baseball, gymnastics, theoretical mathematics, the success or failure of a novel or a play or a sow at the Eastern States Exposition, either. Of course it is a lousy state of affairs.

Wakoski refers, in the same article, to those first books of poetry which are "the sad desperate outcome (and problem) of all of us who teach writing workshops in colleges where it is unfair, bad teaching, poor sportsmanship, and foolish of us to condemn these learning poems." Do you agree with her description of the problems confronting teachers in writing workshops? What has been your experience?

I am musing on Diane's comment about those first books of poetry. I have taught a bunch of workshops in poetry and I have taught them as sympathetically and gently as ever I could. I have not seen, perhaps, the same sad desperate outcome she speaks of. The desperate outcome I *have* observed over and over is that our M.F.A. programs turn out annual crops of talented and ambitious young poets who must then drive milk trucks or deliver the daily paper to stay alive. The problem is not to squelch the would-be poet but to provide him/her with a responsive audience.

When and why did you start writing poetry? Were you ever a student in a writing workshop?

The first poem I ever wrote was on the occasion of the death of a newborn pup when I was eight years old, and it is clearly derivative: "Here lies the runt of a litter of seven / Since he's not on man's earth he must be in dog heaven." In my late twenties I joined a poetry workshop conducted by John Holmes and I put down roots and I put up leaf. It was excruciating and exciting: other people were doing the same thing! It mattered! Thus I came to believe in writing workshops.

In two earlier conversations in Yes, *Adrien Stoutenburg and Colette Inez made the following respective comments: "I confess to considering the 'womanness' or 'maleness' of poetry, or art generally, offensive." "Surely we have been drugged into thinking of 'womanness' in a pejorative light and 'maleness' . . . as the* ne plus ultra *of desirable traits." Will you speak to this point?*

Well, naturally, sex stereotypes are bullshit. We have to be wise enough and secure enough to disclaim them, men and women alike. On the other hand, there is no reason to blur points of view. Some poems demand to be written as "woman poems." And vice versa. We have got to get the pejorative out of them, the pejorative that says admiringly of muscular diction, "that's male." Or that speaks of a love lyric as "peculiarly feminine." Let's learn to say "tough" and "sensitive" without attaching genders to them.

Then where would you place Robert Graves in this discussion? Writing in The White Goddess *he says, "Woman is not a poet: she is either a Muse or she is nothing. This is not to say that a woman should refrain from writing poems; only, that she should write as a woman, not as if she were an honorary man."*

I'm afraid I get a double message from Robert Graves. On the one hand there is this mythic elevation of woman to the rank of goddess and on the other there is this commonsense pronouncement advising the woman poet to be true to herself. I think he has a problem sorting out and would like to have it both ways.

Readers of your poems must be struck, as were we, by the way in which dreams and nightmares appear as vividly recurrent themes, images, settings . . . sometimes even as basic structures. The dark underside of life obviously fascinates you. Was this true of you as a child? Has it developed further as a result of your writing? And would you relate this theme to your poem "Quarry, Pigeon Cove"? [The poem appears in its entirety following Maxine Kumin's reply.]

The dark underside of life fascinated and indeed impaled me as a child, where innocence seemed so often to be shadowed by its twin, depravity. There were some wondrous confusions stalking me then—although raised as a Jew I was sent to convent school for three years; although a modern child I was suckled on Grimm's fairy tales and the nasty moral stories of Struwelpeter. Although I lived in a safe America my father's relatives were going into the ovens. I was a natural candidate for nightmares and I think we never outrun those early shadows. I tend to respect my dreams, perhaps overmuch, as I respect the unconscious and revere the things that arrive in the consciousness unbidden. Almost everything in my poetry in some way comes up through these pipes. "Quarry, Pigeon Cove" in a way illustrates the going down, the risk, and the coming back up unscathed. The special fascination of this dark underside is precisely the absence of any kind of touchstone in it—the atmosphere of the nightmare, of death, without the particulars. A terror looked for but unfound.

Quarry, Pigeon Cove

The dead city waited,
hung upside down in the quarry
without leafmold or pondweed
or a flurry of transparent minnows.
Badlands the color of doeskin
lay open like ancient Egypt.

Frog fins strapped to my feet,
a teaspoon of my own spit in the mask
to keep the glass from fogging,
and the thumbsuck rubber air tube in my mouth
I slid in on my stomach,
a makeshift amphibian.

Whatever the sky was doing
it did now on its own.
The sun shone for the first fifteen feet going down,
then flattened, then petered out.
I hung on the last rung of daylight,
breathing out silver ball bearings,
and looked for the square granite bottom.

I might have swum down looking
soundlessly into nothing,
down stairways and alleys of nothing
until the city took notice
and made me its citizen,
except that life stirred overhead.
I looked up. A dog walked over me.

A dog was swimming and splashing.
Air eggs nested in his fur.
The hairless parts of him bobbled like toys
and the silk of his tail blew past like milkweed.
The licorice pads of his paws
sucked in and out,
making the shapes of kisses.

After that,
the nap of the surface resettled.
Mites danced on both sides of it.
Coming up, my own face seemed beautiful.
The sun broke on my back.

*In another poem, "Sleep," you write, "Actually, over-
lap / is my worst problem. / When the lines that I dangle /
in Walden / are hauled in, / the tail of one thought / is*

found to be hooked / in the mouth of another." Do these lines apply also to the process of writing a poem? Do you often find one poem "spinning off" from another?

In praise of overlap I might say that I often go in search of one thing and come back with another. Yes, there is a definite spin-off from one poem to another, because in the process of narrowing in on a subject a lot of peripheral ideas occur which then struggle to announce themselves. Some of them insist on becoming poems.

An Interview

With Joan Norris

We like to begin our interviews with an autobiographical sketch of the poet. What would you like to tell us about yourself?

I was born in Germantown in Philadelphia in 1925. I grew up in an old Victorian house next door to the convent of the Sisters of Saint Joseph. I went to the convent school during that critical period that Jesuits refer to. Although I'm grateful for some wonderful relationships with the nuns, they instilled in me tremendous anxiety about my immortal soul. I went to high school in Philadelphia and then I came away to Radcliffe. I got a B.A. in history and literature and immediately thereafter married. I went back to study for my Master's and earned the degree six weeks before Jane was born. I didn't do anything with the degree for seven or eight years until Dan, our third child, went off to kindergarten. Then I began teaching at Tufts, half-time, but it was more like a full-time job.

In addition to the Catholic influence, which was very unsettling since I was growing up in a Jewish family, there was a German woman who lived with us. We called

Originally appeared in *Crazy Horse*, no. 16 (Summer 1975). Reprinted by permission.

her Fraulein. She was like a mother to me until I was about seven or eight when she left to get married. My father was one of the biggest pawnbrokers in the city of Philadelphia. That, too, was difficult because my mother always referred to him uncomfortably as a broker. I had three older brothers. I was the center on the football team, but I was only allowed to center the ball. Then I had to run out on the sidelines because I was a girl. I was passionately interested in horses even then and rode every chance I had. I also turned to swimming. It's a true story that I wanted to go to Wellesley because they had a magnificent pool with an underwater observatory room. I was put on their waiting list and went instead to Radcliffe which has a dingy little pool in the basement of the gym, thereby aborting a possible career as an Olympic swimmer.

It is also true that I was invited to join Billy Rose's Aquacade as a summer job in my eighteenth year at the fantastic rate of pay of $125 a week. Although it was very well chaperoned, my father wouldn't let me go. It was just not a decent occupation for a decent girl, traveling around, showing her body in a bathing suit. So I really flunked out as a swimmer and that's how I became a poet. My father lived long enough to see some of my work in print and was terribly proud of me. I think that like many Jewish patriarchs of that generation, he was absolutely astounded by the force of the written word, that you could write something and someone would buy it and print it.

How did you feel when you won the Pulitzer for Up Country*?*

Well, I felt marvelous, very elated and kind of stunned, high on the fun and excitement. I found out I had won when I was at my desk working. Somebody from the Associated Press called and asked me if I had heard that I had won the Pulitzer. I became very suspicious and said, "Who did you say this is?"

You know, I took the Pulitzer and ran. I really couldn't get out of Boston fast enough. For one thing, there's a good deal of publicity attendant upon this. To be catapulted from the relative obscurity and safety of being a poet, who is the smallest frog in the whole literary pond, to being a Pulitzer Prize winner is incredible. The phone rings every minute. People want to come and interview you, or they want something from you. Unsolicited manuscripts begin to arrive. So I was really anxious to get out of the city and get back up here in New Hampshire to my hermitage.

Do you write most of your poems up here at the house in New Hampshire? A lot of them certainly seem to come out of this geography.

Practically all of them have come out of this geography and this state of mind, but I haven't really written very many of them here. I started to be able to write up here last summer. That was the first time that I think I had enough inner tranquillity to be able to balance the out-of-doors and the inner life. I wrote the hermit poems, most of the hermit poems here. Then this summer I've been writing a cycle of horse poems, the Amanda poems. Usually though, the poems about "up country" come back in the city when I'm at my desk in my study.

Are you working on your next volume of poetry now?

Yes, I'm pretty well along too. There were a lot of poems

not included in the *Up Country* volume, perhaps fifteen. I add to them, but I add very slowly. Not everything I write seems to be lasting enough for me to want to include it in a volume.

How do you decide what is lasting enough?

Well, if I'm in doubt, I might try a poem out on people whose opinions I respect. Also, sometimes if you just sit with a poem for a couple of months, it begins to take on, or lose, a certain weight in your own mind and you have no questions about its value.

You write both poetry and fiction. Is there a difference in how you handle each form?

I think when I first started writing poetry, I could require myself to sit down and write a poem. Now I don't do that. I tend to wait for a poem to come to me. I feel that it is at least to some extent a mystical process, because when a poem is working, getting ready to be written, I know it. I know it with an absolute physical sureness. I have what amounts to almost an aura, a real prickle at the base of my neck. I've learned now that when that happens, it's time to get to the desk, or to get to the back of an envelope and the stub of a pencil at least. Then once a poem begins, I can make a total commitment. It doesn't matter if it takes a day, a week, or six weeks. I can stay with it because I have faith in that original impulse. When I'm writing prose, I feel that I'm much more in charge and it is more a matter of pure invention and manipulation. This is not to denigrate the process at all, but if you're writing a novel, you've "thunk up" these people and you've "thunk up" the situations you're going to put them in and the ways in which you are going to resolve whatever conflicts arise. You let the story-telling thing take over. When I'm writing a novel, I never think of it as writing a novel. I think of it as: "Today I will write two pages or else I will spend four hours at the typewriter." That's just the way I do it, and I don't feel safe until I'm a good seventy or eighty or ninety pages into it. Each time I've written a novel, I've dreamed about the people in the novel. That's when I begin to trust the fact that what I'm writing is going to get out of the desk drawer. It's going to become a book. The dream has happened to me each time, and I've learned to trust that reference to the unconscious.

When you're writing your poems, how do you get started?

It varies a great deal. Probably in most cases, I start with either a first line or a pervading rhythm that is in my head. It has happened that I've started with a title or with an ending, so I guess it can really go in almost any direction. Before I wrote "The Hermit Wakes to Bird Sounds," the thing that I had in my head was the part about the oilcan bird, the last image in the poem. Even before I began to write, I knew somehow that image was going to be the closing of the poem. It doesn't usually come that way, but when it does, you want to drive off the road and write it down. That's one of the nice things about a poem. It's small enough to carry around in your head. You can work away at it while you're doing some mechanical things like currying a horse or driving on the turnpike. With the fiction, I found I can't really carry it with me. I can carry a character with me, but not the words.

You've often said that if you were restricted to one form, you'd choose the couplet. Why?

I enjoy the fact that it's so hard. I believe that writing in a rhyme scheme startles you into good metaphor. At least, it works that way for me. It's the form in which to pour the cement of the poem.

Do you keep a journal regularly?

I did keep one for a very long time. It was a working journal—notes about whatever I was writing. It was my habit to sit down at the typewriter with a piece of yellow paper and talk to myself on the typewriter. It was very nice to be able to look back over the notes six or eight weeks later and see where the germs were. I was often able to look back and resolve things when I was blocked. I did this too working on poems. I confided in the journal. There are notes that say I wanted to write a poem about a particular thing and the feelings I was having. It was tremendous to be able to look back a year later and see that, by God, I had done it.

In an interview, Auden mentioned that he first looked at a poem to see what the poet was up to formally. Does your attention focus first on form?

Yes. That is a part of my training as something of a formalist. I'm interested to see what the craft is, because for me the craft and the essence of the poem have to come together. One without the other doesn't really move me; I want them both to happen. I look at the level of the language. A poem that is in form has to operate more than just superficially. It has to really grab me from the point of view of the craft before I'm going to get involved with what the poem is saying. A poem written in free verse is doing something else, and I can meet it on its own terms and like it very much. It isn't relying on the form to elevate the language.

Where do you see yourself falling within the range of American poetry?

I don't know. A lot of people have said that my work is very Frostian, which I take as a high compliment. The poems I really learned by heart and carried around with me were those by Auden, Spender, MacNeice, Karl Shapiro, and Randall Jarrell. That was my generation surfacing out of the Second World War. I think I was very much influenced by their work. The early John Ciardi also. A lot of his poems were very moving to me.

What effect does teaching have on your work?

It's very good for me. I think of it as a discipline—the commitment to meet a class, to keep a workshop alive, stimulating, and ongoing. I feel I get as much as I give. Working with students who are writing poetry is a very feeding thing. I like my students and I like that kind of involvement. I think it keeps me on my toes, probably stimulates me to write more poems than I otherwise would. I'm really very lazy by nature. Intellectually lazy. A bad workshop can be very destructive of the urge to even get on with writing. When I was a freshman in college, I didn't have to take freshman English. It was a huge mistake and I was catapulted into a group of considerably older and more settled students. I gave the instructor a sheaf of poems and about six weeks later he gave them back to me. He had written on the front: "Say it with flowers, but, for God's sake, don't try to write poems." That just closed me off. I didn't try to write another poem for about six years. I was very young, very bemused, very unsure of myself, and very much out of my depth in the situation. But I learned a lesson from it. I learned never to put down a student that way. That's probably the most important lesson I'll ever learn.

An Interview

With Martha George Meek

Our formal subject is poetry as a principle of order in life, when oneself and the world are otherwise chaotic. As we discuss that difficult point where the art and the life of an artist coincide, Kumin reads aloud a quotation from Faulkner as a motto for confessional writers: "If a writer has to rob his mother, he will not hesitate. The 'Ode on a Grecian Urn' is worth any number of old ladies." It is tacked to the bulletin board over her desk, among a collection of family snapshots.

The hermit in the first eight poems of Up Country *is so very alone. I wonder if for you, as well as for the hermit, the tribe, the family, is the last unit in society that can be balanced between order and disorder?*

Yes, I think very definitely.

It's no larger than that?

Well, it's the family and it's the larger family, by extension, of those whom you love. For me, it's certain writers I've been close to and who, in effect, speak the same

---

Reprinted from the *Massachusetts Review,* © 1975 The Massachusetts Review, Inc.

language. Writers are all secret Jews; they all belong to the same tribe. We do talk a kind of private language; well, we tend to talk a lot of shop talk. So there's the commonality of that. There's also the enormous commonality of the fact that to be a writer is to be a solitary. It's to be a hermit; it's to be shut off. Almost any other profession involves some sort of social intercourse with people, you know, with the world around you—medicine and law and so on. But to be a writer is to lock yourself up to do your job. So there's an awful lot of overage, and that's why I think writers like to get together and talk about how terrible it is, how lonely it is, how difficult it is.

This is a professional isolation for you, then, rather than a personal one?

I think by nature I am somthing of a solitary. I mean I'm capable of being sociable and amiable. But I need a lot of quiet; I need a lot of time when I'm not talking. Maybe more than other people do. I suppose what I'm saying is I don't put terribly much store by human nature. I don't think of us as infinitely perfectible as I might have twenty-five years ago. I think we're infinitely depraved, and brutish, and nasty. And this goes back to what you were saying about the family element, the saving nature of the close associations that you can feel within the family or, by extension, within the family of writers, plus a few close, tried-and-true friends.

Does your hermit repudiate modern life?

No, he doesn't repudiate it; he's just a cop-out. And it's a very selfish thing. I have this pervading desire to be totally self-sufficient. I want to have a big vegetable garden we can live off of all year, be really outside the mainstream. It's like living on an island as it is. Last summer I didn't have a car for a large part of the summer, and so, when we needed groceries, I'd go down to town on horseback. That worked out pretty well, except one day the carton of milk spilled onto the five-pound bag of flour in the knapsack, and by the time I got back on the hill, I had a knapsack full of paste. But it was sort of fun. I'd tie my horse to the VFW flagpole and go to market.

Would you do it? Would you leave for good?

The affairs of the world? No, I couldn't. I wish I could. I don't know *how* I feel about it.

In the poem, "September 22nd," you speak of living as a "history of loss."

Yes, "I am tired of this history of loss! / . . . To be reasonable / is to put out the light. / To be reasonable is to let go." There's an old, old essay by Joseph Wood Krutch called "The Phantom of Certitude." He describes all the touchstones of Victorian times when there was the centrality of a belief in the one God and a kind of Calvinist faith in salvation through grace—all of those surenesses that imposed an order in which you could feel that you were growing in a tradition, in which you belonged to an ongoing tradition of the infinite perfectibility of man. I think all those certitudes have been taken from us. "To be reasonable is to let go"; it is really the only sane option that we have.

Do you find any hope for retrieving something from time? I think of "The Hermit Goes Up Attic," and "Cellar Hole in Joppa": There's "no word to keep you by."

Right, right. Except, of course, the word that the poet

records. Always this sense the writer has, a kind of messianic thing: who will tell it if I do not? This is your assignment: to record it, to get it down, to save it for immortality.

Do you think that ultimately language fails us as a means of communication? I'm thinking about references in your poems to dreams, to signs, to messages, as a necessary language that is beyond words.

I have a lot of reverence for what goes on at the dream level in the unconscious—those symbolic events. I have tremendous reverence for raising it up into language, which I think is what it's all about, really. Poetry is so close to the wellspring.

Frequently when you refer to dreams, it's an unbearable truth, though. It's one that's manageable possibly only through dream.

This may very well be so. Want to give me an example? Are you thinking of "The Nightmare Factory"?

Yes, certainly that. That this is a consideration, in fact, that the conscious mind would put aside.

"The Nightmare Factory," as poems so often are, was a way of dealing with something very inchoate and very painful. I wrote it as a way of exorcizing a series of bad dreams about my recently dead father. I developed this fantasy of some distant Detroit-of-the-Soul where all bad dreams are created and that out of the warehouse of goods, we are assigned certain recurrent nightmares that we have to—you know, it's like Conrad. He's talking about the nightmare of one's choice and having to dream it through to the very end, if you remember that; I think it's *Heart of Darkness*. One must descend into the abyss and dream the nightmare of one's choice and dream it through to the very end. I think that's what I was trying to say about those dreams.

If I may quote you once again, from your column in The Writer *this time: "The man who writes out of an inner need is trying to order his corner of the universe; very often the meaning of an experience or an emotion becomes clear to him only in this way."*

Absolutely. That I still believe, very ardently. It happens to me over and over.

The word "order" appears again in the poem, "Stones," in which you speak of the "dark obedient order" of the natural world. Is the crucial order in life an order invented by the writer, or is it a discovered order?

I think that there is an order to be discovered—that's very often true in the natural world—but there is also an order that a human can impose on the chaos of his emotions and the chaos of events. You begin with the chaos of impressions and feelings, this aura that overtakes you, that forces you to write. And, in the process of writing, as you marshal your arguments, as you marshal your metaphors really, as you pound and hammer the poem into shape and into form, the order—the marvelous informing order emerges from it, and it's—I suppose, in a sense, it's in the nature of a religious experience. It must be the same kind of feeling of being shriven that you would have if you were a true believer and you took communion. You feel, to that degree, reborn. Well, ideally, that's what writing a poem does.

The language becomes a part of, as well as a means to, the order which is achieved. Is that it?

It's hard to pin it down. It's what you find out while you're writing. I so often begin in total chaos, not knowing *what* it is I'm doing, just knowing that I have this recurrent phrase, or I have this insistent rhythm, or I have this concept, that I want to fiddle around with. And it isn't until I get the poem out that I find out what it was saying, what I wanted to say. But I don't think that as a creative artist I'm all that conscious; and that gets back to that, you know, for God sakes, Oedipus, not-to-inquire-further thing. I think it's too much part of me. I don't want to know everything, because I'm afraid it will squat on my life and mess up everything that I do unconsciously.

I'm terrified by behavioral scientists. There's a group from Harvard who asked permission to come and sit around while I wrote a poem and see whether they couldn't change the way the poem was built by certain key things they would say or do. I thought that was the most voyeuristic, pornographic idea I'd ever heard of. I hold this process to be sacred; it's between me and my Book of Words, which is in my head. It's almost like inquiring into the mechanism of prayer. If you're really a mystic, or a saint, or somebody who makes things happen by ardently praying them into being, you don't want to investigate exactly what particular line of your incantation works or what particular aspect of your prayer to beseech the Almighty gets through to Him; because then you might come to rely exclusively on those and they might be constantly shifting. You might be all wrong.

You say that in a way it is a religious experience to work with language, as language creates form or order for you.

Well, words are the only "holy" for me. The only sanctity really, for me, is the sanctity of language.

You once wrote about the necessity of being as truthful and "clear" as a natural reticence will allow, even to the point of pain.

That's taken from Marianne Moore. She was a very reticent person. I've largely outgrown my reticence, I think. There was a period in my life when I felt very voyeuristic about what I was writing, daring to deal with interpersonal relationships, old family constellations, and so on. There's a line from a Sexton poem: "The writer is essentially a crook./Out of used furniture he makes a tree." I really love that metaphor because it speaks to the other side of the natural reticence. After all, that is what art should do; create something natural out of all the used-up sticks and bureaus of our lives, the detritus of our lives.

Do you tend to a particular use of form the more intimate the material, the more personal it is?

I generally choose something complex and difficult. The tougher the form the easier it is for me to handle the poem, because the form gives permission to be very gut-honest about feelings. The curious thing for me is that rhyme makes me a better poet. Invariably I feel it does. This is a mystic notion, and I'm not by any stretch a mystic, but it's almost as though I'm not capable of the level of language and metaphor that form enables me to achieve. It raises my language to heights that I wouldn't be up to on my own. When I'm writing free verse, I feel as though I am in Indiana, where it's absolutely flat and you can see the horizon 360 degrees around. You feel as though you have no eyelids, you can't blink. I lose, I have no sense of, the line. There are people who work so easily in this medium; they follow the breath rhythm and the normal pattern of speech. They feel totally at home where I feel totally bewildered. I have to be pretty comfortable about what I'm writing to write a free-verse poem, or else not terribly deeply involved. I almost always put some sort of formal stricture on a deeply felt poem, maybe not rhyme, but at least a stanzaic pattern.

Arbitrary?

In a formal sense it's arbitrary, but the poem finds its form early on, somewhere in the first or second stanza. And again, it's not a conscious thing. You just know the shape the poem's going to take and then you work the poem into that shape. There's that old thing the sculptor is supposed to say when he's carving a horse out of stone: he just chips away the parts that aren't horse.

Once again you're borrowing from a discovered form. You're leaning on it to help you discover it—that form—further.

Right. Right.

Would you say that, in addition to a stanzaic pattern or rhyme scheme, you tend to an understated diction, or a less "poetic" diction, when you're dealing with intimate material?—"The symbol inside this poem is my father's feet. . . ."

Very good example. It's the only time I ever did that, that I'm aware of. That was the hardest poem I ever wrote, as you might well imagine. I wrote it quite a long time after my father was dead. And I *did* use that as a defense between me and the material. It's a way of standing back from the poem and saying: I as an artist am going to tell you a little secret about this poem; I have put a symbol in it. That was a way of getting going on the poem. I don't particularly approve of it; I don't particularly admire poems that are about poetry, for example. I think that some of the worst poems in the English language are written by poets about how they make a poem. I'm usually almost immediately offended by that, but I did do it. It does begin flatly. And it simply tells the details. It's a catalog poem to a large extent. It relies on a thickness of listing things to carry the notion. I wrote that elegy, "Pawnbroker," initially in syllabics as well as rhyme. That's how terrified I was of writing it.

This thickness of detail stands for feelings that you have. For example, in "For My Son on the Highways of His Mind" the listing of the posters on the bedroom wall, the listing of the paraphernalia in the boy's room, are ways of speaking to the mother's feeling about the son. Without having to talk about emotion, you can use this.

You're talking about a defense between yourself and the emotion, rather than an attempt to make it seem genuine?

Well, I don't think that the attempt to make it seem genuine ever enters into it. It's not a conscious thing that happens. I don't ever say to myself, well now, in an attempt to make this seem genuine I will use the following details. I do think, on reflection, that they *are* a kind of defense against the expression of feeling.

Louis Simpson speaks about "the attitudes and tone of prose, in the form of verse," as a description of the volume, Halfway. *Does that seem to you right, or somehow foreign, as a description?*

Well, of course, that was a first book. I have shifted a great deal, and I'm still evolving. That may be true of the poems in *Halfway* but I'm not sure that it's generally true. It's funny that you bring up Simpson because the book that I'm putting together now will be called, *House, Bridge, Fountain, Gate*. It's a direct quote from his partial autobiography, *North of Jamaica*, a lovely book. He says in it: "Poetry is a mixture of thoughts and objects; it is as though things are trying to express themselves through us. It may be, as a poet had said, we are here only to say house, bridge, fountain, gate." Well, that simply fascinated me, because I believe so strongly in the naming and the particularizing of things. I thought that would make a useful title. The poet is Rilke. I'm going to put the German epigraph and then the quote from Simpson at the front of the book. Now, if the naming or the particularity of things is a function of prose more than it is of poetry, to that extent I suppose I do. I think that the one thing that's been consistently true about my poetry is this determination to get authenticity of detail.

That reminds me immediately of "The Spell" and Marianne Moore and the toads.

Do you know, when I wrote that poem I was not thinking of her "imaginary gardens with real toads in them." Not consciously. That's another one of those weird collisions that I tiptoe around the edges of.

What particular writers are you especially fond of?

The things that I like to read are very often the journals and letters, full of despair, of other writers. There's something very comforting in that—also something very voyeuristic. I'm enormously attracted to autobiographies or biographies such as the Bell book on Virginia Woolf.

What about ties with poets writing now?

Anne Sexton was a very close personal friend. I know that sounds odd because we're so different; our voices are so different. But I think every poet needs a poet whose judgment he respects, to try things out on. Anne and I tried things out on each other quite constantly. I think the thing that saved our relationship, which had been going on for eighteen years, was that we didn't intrude on each other. We didn't try ever to moderate or tamper with the other's voice. We were there as a sounding board to say: that's very strained, that image is wrenched, this is dreadful, it's flat, that's an awful rhyme to end on, or whatever it was we said. She was my closest contact. There are some other poets I correspond with and exchange poems with. One, who's really a dear friend of mine, an important pal-of-my-desk, is William Meredith, whose work I admire very much. I think he's one of the finest teachers of poetry; he's such a responsive person. And a good poet. That's the family, the Mafia of the writing world.

There's nothing like a Boston school?

Well, if there is one, I'm not in it, let's put it that way. I don't belong to any group. I really never did—aside from those very first few years when we did have a writers' workshop of John Holmes and George Starbuck and Anne Sexton and me, from time to time. But not since those early days.

Would you say that John Holmes was one of the first to write in the mode of the intimate?

Well, he would turn over in his grave if he'd heard you say so, because he so detested it. He abhorred it, and he abhorred and was frightened of everything that Sexton wrote. He was very opposed to our developing friendship. He thought it would be very destructive for me, and over the years we proved him wrong. I loved John. He was my Christian, academic Daddy. He was responsible for my first teaching job at Tufts where I was a part-time English instructor, equipped, in the eyes of the university, only to teach freshman composition to physical education majors and dental technicians. That was how I began. And John did a superb job of running the workshop. He was a very good teacher. He had a way of eliciting the further detail without interfering with somebody's voice. But he was very much opposed to what is now called confessional poetry. Anne frightened him a great deal because, I think, her hysteria and her suicidal nature reminded him of his first wife. Yet his best poems—the best poems he wrote—were the poems he wrote after we had an ongoing workshop; we were standing on our own legs, all of us, and we were pulling out of him poems more intimate than he had ever written before.

He was writing in response to you then.

We were all writing frantically in response to each other. It was wonderful and terrible all at once. It was a very yeasty and exciting time.

Where did confessional poetry begin?

In a very general way I think the quality of the *I* voice, the *moi* voice, that emerged out of the poetry of the Second World War, was the source that made Lowell, Snodgrass, Sexton, and so on, possible. There was a real loosening that took place in the war, maybe beginning with Shapiro, maybe beginning with Jarrell, maybe beginning God knows where, but somewhere in that group of poets whose poems came out of their experiences in the army or the navy.

What was it in the war?

That it was such a searing and such an intimate experience as well as a collective one. The best poems were the poems that particularized what was going on. I think of the Jarrell poem which has been so widely anthologized, "The Death of the Ball Turret Gunner." It might very well be considered an ancestor to the poems in *Life Studies*. It's a funny link to be making, but it made the voice possible. It was the anguished voice of the soldier that I think of as the forebear of the anguished voice in contemporary poetry.

Even for you as a woman?

Well, I don't know for me as a woman. I didn't really begin to be able to write womanly poems until, let's say, my consciousness was raised by my daughters. I started to grow up at about age thirty. I had a very long childhood, and a long and delayed adolescence. I was programmed into one kind of life, which was to say: get a college degree, get married, and have a family. It was just after the war, and this was what everyone was desperately doing; the tribe *was* seen as the saving centrality in a world that had gone totally awry. And I came to poetry as a way of saving myself because I was so wretchedly discontented, and I felt so guilty about being discontented. It just wasn't enough to be a housewife and a mother. It didn't gratify great chunks of me. I came to poetry purely for self-gratification.

Do you feel that you and Anne Sexton have changed the face of poetry?

I think she has much more than I. She is a very original voice in American poetry. She certainly was responsible in large measure for the outpouring now of what I would call feminist verse. And I don't say feminist at all in a pejorative sense. She made it possible for women to write about the quality of womanhood in a way that just could not have been taken seriously twenty years ago. I don't put myself in that category; I don't know to what degree I may or may not have been an innovator. I think she has very clearly been an innovator, more so, I think, than Lowell. I think she went way beyond his stance.

Do you think that the confessional mode is dying out?

I don't think the confessional voice is dying out. That seems to me part of a long and honorable tradition in poetry: the voice of the *I*. I think we have that in every age in some degree or another.

One hears it asserted so often that with Sylvia Plath's suicide the impulse has been taken to its conclusion.

Certainly that was the logical conclusion to what Sylvia was doing, but it was, ironically, such a death by mistake.

She didn't intend to die?

I think that, as was true with Anne, there is half of the nature that wants to die, that needs to die, that needs to murder the self to get some release from the torment. But at the same time there remains the other part of that being, that wants very much to go on; and it's chancy, it's a steeplechase. Every time you try to die you're taking a risk; you might die, and then again you might be found. The impulse toward suicide is sometimes a sort of substitute punishment. Having made the attempt and then having been hauled back to life, the would-be suicide is in a way satisfied for a time. Death has been served. We've had so many poets die by their own hands. I don't know what the statistics are, poetic suicides as opposed, say, to suicides of bankers. But nonverbal people kill themselves, too. It's just that they haven't articulated their anguish ahead of time.

Do you suppose that's especially a twentieth-century impulse?

No, I don't think it's a twentieth-century impulse; it's just become more plausible with the relaxation of the hold of the church. As soon as you erode the sense of sin—the sin of dying by your own hand—you take away those certitudes we were talking about, and it gets more and more plausible to kill yourself. Like Kirillov in *The Possessed*, the only rational thing you can do is to kill yourself to prove there is no God.

N.B.: Maxine Kumin recently indicated to me that her final comments now seemed abrupt, particularly when read in the context of Anne Sexton's suicide. She wrote: they are too "coldly rational" and angry, although anger has its part in grief. I was reminded of a comment Kumin had made during our earlier discussion of the "history of loss" in a person's life. It is this, she had said, which continually exacts what she once called in Halfway, *"the effort of consent."*

An Interview

At Interlochen

Is everyday life experience the chief influence upon your poetry?

I would say that the distillation of everyday life experiences is exactly what I am trying to particularize and order in poetry.

When you write a poem, do you set down a chunk or block of words and then pare down from that, or do you build line on line?

I set down everything I can think of, everything that flies into my head, even though it may seem terribly digressive. I try to get it all because I'm afraid that if I don't get it all down on the page, it will evanesce and blow away. I tend to get a whole chunk that looks like prose, maybe three or four pages of it. While that's going on, I can already sense that certain of those things are lines, and then the next time through, I can begin to pick out the lines. By the end of the second session with the poem, I can

---

Interview conducted January 6, 1977 at Interlochen Arts Academy, Interlochen, Michigan. Reprinted by permission.

see the order, the stanzaic pattern, if there's going to be one, and so on. It can happen the other way, too. Once in a while a poem will start with a compelling rhythm or line or just a phrase that you can't get rid of, and the poem will come from there.

When you talk about stanza patterns, do you mean the traditional one that someone like Auden would use?

Yes. I love Auden's work, and I think I learned a tremendous amount by imitating him, by deliberately cultivating that easy conversational tone of voice in which his poems are written, and by imitating to the best of my ability that deceptively easy-looking rhymed quatrain. The shorter the number of feet in a line the harder, of course, it is to work inside it. And he did so beautifully those short lines, some of them trimeter, some of them tetrameter.

Can you hinder your own work if you make too many drafts of it or rummage through it too many times?

Yes, I think you can. It's very hard to know when to stop because, you see, a poem is not like a watercolor. If you're painting a watercolor, you either have something in twenty minutes or you tear it up because you just "muddy" it if you go back over it. But you never lose anything by revising and recasting and trying different approaches, and so the problem is likely that with too much revision, the poem doesn't get finished. And yet, in truth, I would have to say immodestly that I think I always know when a poem is finished for me. It's taken me a long time to learn that, but I don't think I will worry a poem beyond its completion.

How do you begin your poems? Do you "think" them for a while before you write them down, do you sit down and try to write them, or do you get a line and start writing to see where it goes?

I don't think them before I write them, I know, because I'm always startled and often perplexed at what is building. I tend to just sit down and let it go. I think it starts in some very inchoate place, and the whole process of writing the poem is a process of elucidation. It's an attempt to find the truth for that particular corner of the universe.

You don't think you could force it, though.

Well, I did in the olden days when I was learning, when I was a beginner poet. I am a strong believer in the exercise poem and the workshop poem as a way of learning craft. I'm also old fashioned enough to believe that it's very useful in workshop where the group dynamics are good and people are really constructive and loving with one another to write poems in common. I've worked with classes where we've written a sonnet in an hour, all of us together, to a predetermined end rhyme. Or I often use the device of group assignments where everybody has to write a dream poem or everybody has to write a descriptive poem of a person—you know, that kind of thing. And I think those things are useful. Sometimes exercise poems can turn into real true poems, and even if they don't, they've taught you something.

Have you ever given up on a poem?

Oh yes, lots of times. I have a great big box, a box that

shirts used to come back from the laundry in before plastic bags were popular. That's my bone pile, and all the little snippets that failed and the aborted poems and stuff are in that. Don't ever throw those away because there'll be some wonderful phrase, maybe just two words in that box, but they're there. Going through your bone pile is often a very useful way to get started on a new poem. You can dip in there and find something that you couldn't deal with six months before. And suddenly it will right itself. That's a very mystic experience. I had once put away a poem in rhyming couplets. I think I had six or eight rhyming couplets. I had no way—no knowledge of how to complete this poem. I wrote probably forty-five wrong endings, and I put it away in the bone pile. Two years later I took it out, and I read through it. What came was like automatic writing. I just wrote the last three couplets, and there it was. It was an incredible experience. So this happens. It happens pretty frequently to a lot of poets.

How far do you think you should analyze a poem?

That's a very good question. Not quite to the point of pain. There is something known as "creeping exegesis" which is dissecting the poor poem until it wriggles around and is eventually killed. When I was young a lot of Robert Frost was killed for me in precisely that way. Almost all of Shakespeare was murdered in my high school days, and it was a long time before I could go back to him with anything other than a leaden sense of duty. Close examination of the text to understand what the poem is doing and how it works is fine because that heightens the poem, makes it much more meaningful. And then there has to be a point where the poem is something aesthetic, and you bring your own aesthetic judgment to bear on it.

In writing poems do you have a duty to yourself or to something else?

I'm really not sure. I'm not sure it's duty. I honestly think it's obsession. I mean, I don't think that I write poetry necessarily because I want to. I write it because I feel compelled. It's something I can't get away from—it's in me.

Have you ever felt that you've not been totally honest in a poem?

Well, it's hard to give an honest answer because there is a quality in poetry that I like to call poetic tact. There are some things that go unspoken. And a tremendous part of the punch of a good poem is in understatement, rather than hyperbole. Hyperbole has been so overused that it, like cliché, has lost its power to evoke feeling. If by understating, one is being not totally honest about the subject, then I guess I would have to say, yes, that I have not been totally honest in poems. But as far as telling the truth as I see it, I would have to say that I think I am always as honest as I can be.

Does your reference to I *in a poem relate the character's feelings or your own personal feelings?*

It can be either and it can be a little of both, because the *I* is the persona that the poet is hiding behind. There's an ancient and honorable tradition in poetry to use the *I*, or as the French call it, *le moi*, as a vehicle for conveying emotion or fact or whatever. Sometimes it can be very much a persona poem, and sometimes it can be quite an autobiographical poem.

Were you hiding behind the male persona in the hermit poems?

Yes. If I were writing them today, I would not employ the male persona. But when I was writing them I did not think that anyone could take a female hermit seriously, so I invented the hermit who, of course, is me. In the Amanda poems, however, that's no persona; there's nothing between me and the material.

Do you have to give yourself time between poems for something to build up?

Sometimes there's a great spate of them. Recently I was at the University of Arkansas doing a writers' workshop for a week, and I went from there to Washington for National Endowment meetings and then to read at the Folger Library. While I was in Arkansas I stayed in a dreary motel. It fronted right on a parking lot, and cars roared in and out at all hours. I was in that room quite a lot between student conferences and so on, and I started having nightmares. When I'm on the road I frequently have bad travel dreams in which everything is going wrong back at the farm. I wrote a whole poem in that motel, a poem I'm delighted with: in fact the *New Yorker* just bought it. I worked on it a little more after I got home because I cannot see in longhand what the poem will look like on the page. Then, while I was in Washington, I was taken to the King Tut Exhibit. It was hot and crowded, but the experience was overwhelming.

I could have spent three days peering into those cases. And flying back to Boston I started another poem on the back of an airline ticket. It's called "Remembering Pearl Harbor," and it's about seeing the King Tut Exhibit on Pearl Harbor Day. Now that may seem a very tenuous connection to you; it did to me. I could not find the connective link for the longest time. I sent the poem to a young poet friend of mine, someone who was not yet born when Pearl Harbor was bombed. I asked her whether it worked for her, because I was afraid that maybe it was just a generational poem. And she explained to me what the connections were. Now, of course, I see them, but I didn't see them while I was writing it. So I suddenly got those two poems, just all very unexpectedly. I hadn't gone seeking them, and there they were.

You have talked about being worried in Fayetteville— about the farm and having these nightmares. Have your husband and your children also affected your writing?

Oh, yes, very much so. I've written a great deal about family relationships. Although the children have grown and gone, they turn up in things.

Has your early family life greatly affected your later po- etry, or do you feel it affected more your earlier poetry?

I think I'd have to say it's about fifty-fifty. You never get rid of family relationships, you know. I will always have a mother. My mother is eighty-two, but I still have her and, therefore, I'm still a child— I'm still a daughter. Such things carry through the generations, I think, for- ever. My father, for example, has been dead for fourteen years, but he still turns up in my dreams. It's astonishing how we are never really free of these relationships, of our position in the family. We carry these with us either as a burden or a joy.

You've spoken before about a kind of falling out with the whole religious experience. Do you think that poetry is in some way a fulfillment of some sort of spiritual need?

You really are asking me very hard questions. I don't know how to answer that. I call myself an agnostic. I do not really have any faith, any coherent religious faith, and yet the one thing in my life that I feel passionate and evangelical about is poetry. I want to contribute to its well-being and to its future. And I suppose that speaking about the way poems occur is, if you read William James, something like the quality of a religious experience for me.

Do you worry about how your readers are going to read your poems?

I try not to worry about them. I try to put that out of my head, because if you once start worrying about how readers are going to react, it's a very short step from that to worrying about how listeners are going to perceive your poems, and from there it's only a half step to trying very hard to amuse and titillate them. Then pretty soon you are just pandering to an audience, and you're no longer a poet; you're just a performer. So you have to have some convictions about the worth of what you're doing, artistically. You cannot think of it as something that you're doing for the year 1977, but instead as something you hope will outlast you.

How much do you think a reader has to take to one of your poems to get something from it?

Well, I think he has to be reasonably intelligent and reasonably educated and reasonably sympathetic. At least that's what I would like.

Should you worry if he read it differently from what you intended?

I would probably be a little sorry, but if he got something out of it, that would be good. Poetry's a very fragile art form. I think it's the most fragile of all, and I think it requires the most preparation. There are so many dunces listening to music in this world and getting little from it that it rather appalls you when you stop to think. Everybody takes his little rug and cuddles up in pairs to hear Arthur Fiedler conduct the Boston Pops. But somehow more people listen to music with less comprehension than people read poetry. In other words, people don't bother to come to poetry unless they can work it through.

Do you like giving poetry readings?

I do not really like giving readings. I don't panic about them the way I once did. I used to endure agonizing anxieties before a reading, and I know a lot of poets who still do. For some mysterious reason, which I hope will never be clear to me, the terrible terror went away, just gradually eroded over a period of years of forcing myself to do it. What I'm left with is a generalized case of the jitters before I go on. And once I'm into a reading, if the audience is receptive, I could almost say I'm enjoying it—almost. But it's not something I would choose, occupationally. I have to be honest and say I do it for money. And there are some readings—at the Folger, the YMHA in New York, or the Library of Congress—readings like that to which one simply does not say no. You go and you do it.

Do you believe that a reading adds something to poetry?

Definitely, definitely. Poetry is an oral tradition. I think it immensely enhances the person's poetry for an audience to hear it in the poet's voice. I look back on occasions when I heard poets read (and I heard every one I could get to), and I can remember hearing Robert Frost in Sever Hall at Harvard when people were sitting six deep on the windowsills—there were thousands of people in that hall. I heard Auden innumerable times. I heard John Crowe Ransom read his own poetry in his last years, and that was a fantastic experience. I can never again read a Ransom poem without hearing that marvelously rich southern voice, very controlled, used like an instrument. It gave me goosebumps. His poems gave me goosebumps to begin with, but now they're just immensely deepened. And I think I have felt that way about every poet I've heard read well. Marianne Moore read badly. She could not project her voice and she could not look at the audience, but even so it was exciting to see this great lady in her black cape and her big tricorne black hat. Some of these poets were great personages; some of them were real performers. I'm not sure I like the histrionic performances, but I like to hear the poet's breaks, where the emphasis is, where in the poet's head the interior of the line breaks, etc.

How does your poetry touch your fiction or your fiction touch your poetry?

All over the place and in many ways. I tend to steal from myself. The compass of the poem is so small and so demanding, you have to be so selective, and there are so many things that get left out that you feel cheated. So you take all those things that you couldn't really expatiate upon and they get into the fiction. If you read *The Designated Heir*, my new novel, you'll find probably lots and lots of points in which the text touches the poems and maybe even some recurring phrases, lifted, pirated out of poems that then I could go on with in fiction.

How much do you think a young writer should write? Should he write only as much as he feels like, or should he force himself to keep writing?

I think there's a real value to forcing. I do not think it hurts at all to write to assignment. Granted, the piece that you write for an assignment may not be as good as the piece that you wrote when you were moved to do so, but it will train something in you. Maybe it only trains your typing, but it does train something. I have heard fiction writers say that if you want to learn to write dialogue, get a volume of Hemingway's short stories, sit down at the typewriter, and copy, copy. Just type the text. Now that may sound ludicrous to you, but several things happen. In the first place, you learn how to punctuate conversation. In the second place, you begin to learn how terse and direct conversation can be on the page and how few attributives you really do need. You get out of all of those awful Tom Swifties: "he said, lovingly," "she said, languidly," "she said, contritely," etc. So you learn something about the concision and the terseness of style for which Hemingway is justifiably famous.

What advice would you give to young writers? What sort of reading should they do?

It's a good idea to get in the habit of keeping a notebook or journal, private or semiprivate. Get in the habit of jotting down states of mind or weather reports. It's habit forming and it's good. Also, I do not think anybody becomes a writer who is not a huge reader, omnivorous and wide-ranging. You have to be somebody who's turned on by reading. You have to love words, and you have to be willing to take lots of risks with words, and be willing to write really bad stuff in order to get to the good stuff. You only grow by doing, I think.

An Interview

With Karla Hammond

In your interview with Yes *magazine, the editors mention John Ciardi's reference to your observing things with a "master eye." Would you say that you approach writing with curiosity and distance?*

I don't know. I particularly observe things in nature because they interest me, but I don't think of it as observing. What I'm always after is to get the facts: to be true to the actuality. I had a student once say to me very crossly, "what you want in poems is lots of furniture." It's true; that's what I do want. I mean I want the furniture to kind of subsume the poem so that it doesn't have to project any message. The furniture then becomes the poem. Need for distance? Yes, psychic distance. Wordsworth said it—"emotion recollected in tranquility." It's very hard to write about the recent past. You've got to be able to back off from that in order to deal with it. I know that it's a mistake to try to read to an audience poems that you don't have sufficient psychic distance on, even though you may have been ready to write them. Sometimes you're not ready to read them aloud.

Reprinted from the *Western Humanities Review* 33, no. 1 (Winter 1979). Copyright © 1979 Western Humanities Review.

Is all poetry, for you, then autobiography?

To a certain extent. It doesn't have to be about the self, but it has self invested in it or else it couldn't get written.

Generally, does your poetry address collective experience or is it primarily the expression of a personal mythology?

No. I think that it is much more the expression of the personal mythology. There's the desire that the two will overlap, the hope that the poem draws on some sort of unconscious, collective, archetypal thing so that myth and experience will cohere.

Is your tribal poetry, so designated, ritualistic?

I feel I have a strong sense of tribe and ancestor, an ancestor worship or desire to find out about my roots. I think that if you have Eastern European roots, as I do, and if you are a product of immigrant grandparents or great grandparents who left the Old World behind, you have a chronic sense of unfulfillment.

A number of your poems center on rural experience. Do you regard yourself a regional poet?

Yes, I guess I *am* a regional poet. At least I've *become* one. I'm usually described as a pastoral, or a New England poet. I have been twitted with the epithet "Roberta Frost," which is not a bad thing to be. I've written a number of poems that center on rural experience, but I've also written many tribal poems—poems about family and familial relationships.

How influential were either of your parents in your early writing? Did they encourage your interest? Were either of them writers?

No one in the immediate family was influential in my early writing. My parents didn't discourage me, but neither was a writer.

If not your parents, what early factors led you to write?

This is just to repeat what I've said elsewhere. I think the reason I wrote as a child was to work out unhappinesses and feelings of isolation and solitude. I believe that's true for most writers. There is the old cliché: Behind every writer stands an unhappy childhood.

What sensibility do you look for in poetry? You've praised Heather McHugh's work and I wonder if you could speak about the positive qualities manifest in her poetry?

I think that I look for in poetry what is congenial to my tastes: a freedom from abstraction, a focus on detail, a piling up of specificities to elicit an emotional response, a sensibility that is attractive, and an attitude—a world view—that approximates my own or deepens in some way my own appreciations. Now that's very vague. I like Heather McHugh's work because it's wild but it's very well rooted in reality. She can be quite surreal and fantastic and hypermanic in the poems, but they are well tied into the frame. She's a very original voice and I like what she's doing.

Do you regard poetry as a "trap"—as a means of "snar-

ing" or enmeshing another's attention or imagination where metaphors and similes are "tricks?"

I don't know that I think of metaphors and similes as tricks because they seem to come so naturally. Nemerov says that metaphor stands between a thing and a thought. That's really a solid definition because metaphor is sort of a halfway place between a tangible item and an attitude, as it were. But metaphor is what poetry is all about. Without image, metaphor, simile, it seems to me, there is no poetry. I'm not at all hospitable to the new flat school of poetry. It bores me right out of my skull.

Anne Sexton has said that "craft is a trick you make up to let you write the poem." Would you agree?

Yes. You see, we learned our craft in the same school. We learned the whole gamut of rhyme scheme, metrical devices, syllabics, multisyllabic rhymes—which she was so good at—and so on. We both felt that using these tricks of craft, as she calls them, heightened the level of language of which the poet was then capable. This is certainly true for me. I know that I write better poems in form—within the exigencies of a rhyme scheme and a metrical pattern—than I do in the looser line of free verse. Others can argue this point, claiming that free verse is a form and as such is just as formal. But for me it isn't. Maybe it's because I'm so compulsive that I need the shape to hold me together. The harder—that is, the more psychically difficult—the poem is to write, the more likely I am to choose a difficult pattern to pound it into. This is true because, paradoxically, the difficulty frees me to be more honest and more direct. It is Yeats's "The fascination of what's difficult." I love working with rhyme. I don't mean a bang-bang, tom-tom rhythm, but rhymes that don't obtrude, rhymes that don't announce themselves but are there. They do become a kind of intellectual game. They fall very pleasantly on the ear and I think they enhance what the poem is saying.

Do you feel any affinity to such poets as William Stafford, Jim Harrison, May Sarton, A. R. Ammons, Robert Bly because of their similar poetic concerns and themes?

Only in a distant way, which is not to say I don't admire this list. I do enjoy reading these poets and I know Bill Stafford's work best. Ammons's work is more lyrical and mystical than mine. I feel tremendous affinity to what other women are writing at this time in my life and I find that I'm very interested in what women are writing, what they are thinking about and dealing with.

Do you believe there are different problems with which male and female poets have to contend?

I don't know whether they're different qualitatively— they're just different mind sets or different social attitudes. The problems that the writer faces are the same. I think that it is dangerous to set up these distinctions, male and female, and make scapegoats of them. I'm a great one for blurring the distinctions and the stereotypes, anyhow. I feel very strongly that that's the direction in which we've got to move.

Would you comment on the following statement?

The woman who needs to create works of art is born with a kind of psychic tension in her which drives her unmercifully to find a way to balance, to make herself whole. Every hu-

man being has this need: in the artist it is mandatory. Unable to fulfill it, he goes mad. But when the artist is a woman she fulfills it at the expense *of herself as a* woman.
[*May Sarton*, Mrs. Stevens Hears the Mermaids Singing]

I'm afraid that I don't agree with May Sarton. I don't think that a woman fulfills her need to write at the *expense* of herself as a woman. I think that the creative process is androgynous. It has nothing to do with gender, which is not to say that there aren't womanly poems as opposed to male type poems. Of course there are. When a woman writes about the quality of being female, then she writes a womanly poem. I don't see, however, why that should drive a woman to the brink anymore than it drives a man. Why at the *expense* of herself as a woman? She obviously speaks out of her own self, but why isn't that profit rather than loss? Why should it be any different for a man? The commitment is the same; it's *human*.

Is writing poetry risk taking?

I think of just being alive as risk taking. Poetry writing is risk taking in the most metaphorical sense. There are the physical risk takers—steeplechasers and such—and then there are the metaphorical risk takers. You don't put your life on the line with a poem. You may put your psychic life on the line, but I think that we shouldn't lose sight of the distinction.

Gwen Head has a poem in which a line reads, "To know does violence"—a theme not unlike one of yours. To what extent do you regard poetry as a means of revising pain in a context which, while you may not be able to completely accept it, you can understand it?

I do regard poetry as a way of dealing with pain, a way of working through it. That is to say, I regard poetry as therapeutic to some degree. For the most part, we write out of a desperate need to come to terms with situations. Frequently, that is the motivating force for the poem. I also believe very strongly that poetry is essentially elegiac in its nature, and that all poems are in one sense or another elegies. Love poems, particularly, are elegies because if we were not informed with a sense of dying we wouldn't be moved to write love poems. The best love poems have that element of longing in them: that either they'll lose that love or that time will take it away. Behind the love poem there's always that sense of regret, that sense of doom.

> *Better to come*
> *whole on mermaids or great snakes,*
> *credible things, sirens*
> *and Circes, than be seduced by pain.*
> *["The Heron,"* Halfway*]*

Is this a poetic coat of arms?

> *For suffering there is no quantum.*
> *["The Amsterdam Poem,"* The Nightmare Factory*]*

Is this quotation an extension of the first?

I would disclaim these as a poetic coat of arms. "The Heron" is one of the poems that I would prefer to disown. It's so full of purple rhetoric; it was a young poet's poem. Even in that poem, however, you see my empathy with the maimed animal—in this case the wounded heron. That empathy still very much pervades my sensibilities. It always seems especially cruel to me when an animal suffers because an animal has no way of dealing with it. As for the line, "For suffering there is no quantum," in other words, there's no way of measuring how much suffering anyone feels. The poem talks about what the Dutch went through during the German Occupation. Fifty thousand people, I believe, starved to death in Amsterdam. Some incredible figure like that. The rest of the populace survived by eating all of its pigeons, stray dogs, etc. They'd begun quite literally to eat the rats that came up out of the river. What I was saying is that *I* seem to be the one who can't forgive. The people who actually endured the suffering, came through the experience, picked up their lives again, and have assumed this attitude of normalcy. That was the incredible thing about being in Amsterdam and going to the Anne Frank house, now a national shrine, and so on. I don't know what constitutes suffering any more than I know what constitutes the healing process. I don't think I've explained it very well, but maybe it helps.

Is "Bedtime Story" a personal statement of social commentary or simply a poem for a daughter whose origins are historical? Do you regard any of your poems as "protest" poems?

Both. It's a tribal poem in the prime sense because it reaches back into those historical facts that I would want to keep alive. A couple of my poems are quite overtly "protest" poems. For example, see "Heaven as Anus." I tried it out on my students when I was teaching at the Newton College of the Sacred Heart and I remember one of them said afterward, "Poor God, everyone blames everything on Him." I thought that was a marvelous kind of compassion to have. "Heaven as Anus" is obviously an antiwar, anti-behavior modification poem. "The Summer of the Watergate Hearings" is an angry political poem, to take another, but these are not the kinds of poems I generally write. Most polemical poetry is so shrill that it makes me uncomfortable and I think that the poetry frequently gets lost in the message. I think, however, that one can say things of social importance in poetry, and I defend the right of the poet to preach, even if I prefer not to.

"I cannot convert / to 1966." [*"The Paris Poem,"* The Nightmare Factory] *Is this both a personal and political statement? A refusal to renounce the past?*

Yes. I was still locked in the Nazi Occupation of Paris. I was reading the book, *Is Paris Burning?*, during my first trip to Europe and I was just stunned by everything I saw around me.

> *I, a lapsed pacifist fallen from grace*
> *puffed with Darwinian pieties for killing, . . .*
> *[*"Woodchucks,"* Up Country]*

This quotation in its political implications seems to be a message central to your other poems. Is it a sense of collective guilt? Does it go back to the Anne Frank passage as the last two lines: "If only they'd all consented to die unseen / gassed underground the quiet Nazi way" suggest? Could you explain what you mean by "Darwinian pieties?"

Yes. "I, a lapsed pacifist fallen from grace" from the Woodchuck poem is a kind of overstatement, a self-mocking statement. But it's really true, this sense of collective guilt. It does go back to the Anne Frank poem,

"The Amsterdam Poem". These lines were the most terrible, chilling ending that I could come up with. Are you asking me to define "Darwinian pieties for killing?" It's simply the survival of the fittest; the Darwinian justification for shooting woodchucks is that they eat the garden; we depend on the garden. Therefore, in order to survive, we have to exterminate woodchucks.

What are your impressions of the concentration camp poems recently written (Heyen's, Snodgrass's) or fiction (Susan Fromberg Schaeffer's Anya)?

It's interesting that you mention Bill Heyen. And I was just talking to someone last night about Snodgrass's new book [*In the Führer Bunker*]. I thought Heyen's book was remarkable. I identified so with that, having lived through the war as a small child full of guilt for being a safe American Jew. I had instant empathy for Bill Heyen living through the war as a safe WASP German and for his sense of guilt and the kinds of punishments that were visited on him. W. D. Snodgrass's book represents a terrifying act of the imagination. I find all of these things very moving and I find them important. They're an integral part of the literature of our time. I, for one, feel very strongly that every high school kid ought, under penalty of decapitation, to be forced to read these texts, and to see Ophuls's films on the subject. I'm so afraid that the history and the lessons will be lost.

Reading "Haman's Ears," I'm reminded of a statement of Stanley Kunitz's: "There's hope for you as long as you keep on being terrified by history."

You're reading an old poem of mine. "Haman's Ears" is

one that I haven't looked at for ages. Of course, everything Stanley Kunitz says seems exceedingly wise to me. He said a parallel thing, something I hung over my desk for the longest time, that without history there can be no poetry. Without a past, there is no present. I very much agree. He also said that youth is not a state of genius, it's a biological condition. That's a lovely crusty remark to have made as one gets older.

Do you regard your poetry as particularly prophetic: "Before disasters there are omens" ["History Lesson"] or "To be reasonable / is to put out the light. / To be reasonable is to let go" ["September 22nd"]?

In a sense I think I do. Of course, that's the history of the poet, the poet regarded as shaman, a kind of Tiresias figure through the ages.

Do you regard poetry as mystical: the act of writing in part an act of worship?

Yes. I regard the act of writing in part an act of worship.

Could you describe your process of writing? Do you work at a desk? Do you record in longhand, by typewriter?

All writers love to talk about their writing habits. It's like a coalition of carpenters discussing tools. Yes, I write at a desk. I write on a typewriter. Right now I'm doing an article for *Country Journal*. What I generally do is what you see there [pointing]. I get halfway down the page then I pull it out of the machine and start scribbling all over it in longhand. I spend a lot of time retyping things because it seems to me that everytime I retype something, something else changes—transmutes. I write on yellow paper because I'm intimidated by white paper. It's too formal.

Then do you think of revision as a creative impetus?

To a certain extent, yes; but revision is really a desperate process. It's a desperate desire to make it better—make it right, make it work—so that it can last. That's the only reason to revise. To make it strong enough so that it will be around after you're gone.

Do you keep all drafts until the poem is in its final form? Do you revise after publication?

I do keep all drafts. I even try to number them. I usually forget to, but sometimes afterward I can go back and number just so I can see. It's very interesting to me how the poem began because it usually comes on in such a mysterious way compared to the way it finishes. Sometimes two or three poems will begin on that first page and they get dropped. Sometimes if you go back you can pick those up and find them later. I don't revise after publication largely because I'm too lazy or too discomfitted with the way the poem looks. There are poems in my first book that I would cheerfully shred and keep from the public eye forever.

Which poem has required the greatest revision?

I'm not sure. So many of my poems will go through thirty-five or forty different permutations. It's not at all unusual for me. I think "For My Son on the Highways of His Mind" was a really difficult poem to work, mostly because it took me so long to realize that I would have to write the expository parts in that iambic pentameter line and then just alternate the refrains. Initially, I saw that poem as a matching poem to a poem in my first book called "Poem for My Son" (about my son at the age of six learning to swim). The early poem is very derivative, based exactly on an Auden stanza if you look at it. I wanted to reproduce that stanza pattern, but discovered that there was just no way to compress all the material, all the cataloging. So I wasted an awful lot of time and effort. After I finally hit on the pattern for the poem it became somewhat easier to write. I've kept all the work sheets for that and they're a great thick pile.

Are you aware of any mnemonic devices in writing? Any inhibitory factors? Superstitions?

Anything that works is good. I'm not superstitious about these devices. There are inhibitory factors. If I think that I'm overheard or that there's a lack of privacy or if the material I'm working on is too close to the bone in terms of family or other relationships that would get in the way, it's difficult to work.

Are there poems you've shelved indefinitely? Some you'll never finish?

Yes. There are some, I guess, I will never finish. But one, in particular, I can point to with pride because it did finally work out. It's called "Notes on a Blizzard." I have the original work sheets for that poem. On one of them there are all of these lines and notations in Anne's handwriting where she was trying—it was in free verse and I was so worried about line breaks—and she was trying to explain to me how she decides when a line should push out and when it should push in. Of course, it was a totally individual, idiosyncratic thing. Didn't make any sense at all to me, nor did I go, finally, with the loosened line, but it made me feel good to see her handwriting and her labor. I took the bones of that poem with me and worked on it at Princeton in the spring semester. I had a lovely, big, bare office there and wonderful breathing space in which to work. What saved "Notes on a Blizzard" was the appearance of wild turkeys on our property this past winter. That became the thread. It was the missing little scarlet thread that could get stitched through the poem and bring it down through the jelly beans to the end. Looking back, I saw that I first started the poem in the diary form and the only line that I retained from the first work sheet through every draft was "Only liars keep diaries." So the process, as I said, really is mysterious.

Previous to Up Country *did you have a sense of thematic continuity?*

No, I don't think so. I've gone through certain phases in my writing. In my early poems I wrote a great deal about being a Jew in a Christian culture and about the confusion that pervades almost all these poems you've mentioned. I did grow up next door to a convent and did go to convent school because it was so convenient. My parents sent me there to attend nursery school and kindergarten. I think I stayed through first or second grade. To a child who is looking for absolutes these two opposing views of the world are terribly confusing. You really come out of the womb looking for absolute simple truths to guide by, and you spend the rest of your life learning that just staying alive is a compliment. That's why I wrote so much about these ambivalent feelings. "Halfway," "Mother Rosarine," "Sisyphus," "Bedtime Story," "Haman's Ears"—those early poems all take one kind of stance. By the time we get to "Living Alone with Jesus" and "Young Nun at Bread Loaf" I think I'm much more at home with the reality of it. I'm more comfortable with my role and I'm able to be a lot more wry about it. Living in Kentucky in a hardshell-Baptist area where I was writer-in-residence was an exotic experience, more exotic, say, than going to live in Paris. I was more at home in Paris than I was, initially, in Kentucky. It was a fascinating experience, but I could be detached: I could stand back from it. There was this pervasive, Pentacostal Evangelical Baptist proselytism: "Are you saved? Repent, Repent! Jesus is the answer!" everywhere you turned. I had never seen so much of Jesus or seen him taken so personally. I saw much more of Jesus in Kentucky, really, than I saw of Jesus in the convent.

Have you consciously experimented with different styles? Presently do you see the shape of another manuscript? Is there a pervasive theme in this new work?

I have consciously experimented with different styles, but I've found that it doesn't really work to try to change what we might call outlook or voice. Style is fairly malleable, but voice, I think, is not. Right now I'm putting the finishing touches on the manuscript, *The Retrieval System*. Viking will publish this book in May of 1978. With these poems I consciously set out—I wanted to write something I hadn't written before that would give a little more modeling to the book. I discovered that I just couldn't do it. The new poems that came were simply further developments, offshoots, of the voice that's already established in the book. A pervasive theme?—yes, I think there is. I regret to say that I think the theme is growing older, facing death, the search for the soul. It's a metaphorical search, but I keep writing about the lowercase soul as though it were an actual organ in the body for which I'm looking. That tickles my imagination. It amuses me intellectually at the same time that it expresses a real driving need. So I've let those soul poems go on and on and they do keep turning up. The development of one's voice, point of view, or whatever you're going to call it, is for the most part unconscious. I think, at a given point in time, you can stand back from your work and see what's happened to it, but it's pretty difficult to deliberately shape what you're doing.

Are you working on a prose manuscript? Have you done any critical work aside from reviewing?

I'm finishing, I hope I'm finishing, a collection of short stories that Viking is also publishing. I'm about two-thirds of the way through it. I haven't really done any critical work aside from reviewing, only an essay here and there. I write in a lot of other genres. I write children's books. I wrote four jointly with Anne and sixteen on my own. I'm doing some prose pieces on horses now.

You mentioned reviewing. Do you enjoy it?

Not at all. There are some poets who do it for a living and do it really well—people like Stanley Plumly, for example, Donald Hall, and Marvin Bell. I'm very uneasy doing it. The only reviews I can bear to do are books that I feel absolutely totally enthusiastic about, like Philip Larkin's *High Windows*. I did review that for Maggie

Manning at the *Globe*. But I don't like to be put in the position of hatcheting a book. I'd rather turn it down than have to do that. So you can see, I'm not cut out for making value judgments.

Have you done any translating?

Yes. My daughter Judith and I have been translating a young Belgian poet who writes in French. Of course, Belgian French is different from French French. There are a great many idioms of which a Parisian would have no knowledge. It's a very interesting collaboration—kind of a three-way collaboration because André speaks a creditable bookish English and my French is a very proper bookish French. My daughter, however, who lives in Brussels and is an interpreter for the Common Market, is very at home with the idiom and the colloquialisms. André came over last summer to visit and it gave me a chance to see if we had caught the tone that he wished. Were we just approximating or were we absolutely wrong? Had we missed the pun? He resorts to an enormous amount of word play, making it difficult to translate him closely. Translating is like doing a crossword puzzle, or better: it's like doing a double-crostic puzzle, which is more fun. It's a wonderful thing to have to occupy you when your own work goes dry because it's a more mechanical process, although it requires a great deal of creativity. I'm not really good at languages. In fact, it grieves me. I've had four years of college Russian and although I've had six years of furious academic layers of French, my conversational French is stilted. I get along, but it will always be stilted. It's too late for me now to develop the kind of ear that, say, Judy has. She's so fluent. She's just as fluent in German and almost as fluent in Dutch. It's like being musical. The gift for language is a genetic thing. I hope that we can get our young man published on this side of the Atlantic. He's anticlerical, iconoclastic, defensively and blatantly and frequently very funnily homosexual. He's written all of these onanistic poems that are titled "Masturbation I," "II," "III," "IV." I'm not sure that we're going to get him published, but we're working on it.

Muriel Rukeyser has said that she confronts dry periods by working in translation. Richard Wilbur calls this risky business because it can serve as a means of distraction. How do you feel?

I see that Muriel Rukeyser feels very much about translating as I do. Wilbur says that it can serve as a means of distraction from your own work. Yes, that is a definite risk, but so can everything. I can find more ways to evade getting down to business than a centipede has legs. It's just astonishing the things that I can suddenly decide need doing that have nothing to do with writing. I'm a terrible jock and I tend to escape mental work by plunging into physical activity, splitting wood, clearing brush, gathering mushrooms.

Have you ever had the desire to pursue a career other than writing?

Yes. I was going to be an Olympic swimmer, in the first instance, at sixteen. Now, if I could shed twenty or thirty years, I'd like to be a professional horse trainer.

Would you recommend poetry as a career? In discussing its advantages and disadvantages, what advice would you offer a young poet?

I would not recommend poetry as a career. In the first place, it's impossible in this time and place—in this culture—to make poetry a career. The writing of poetry is one thing. It's an obsession, the scratching of a divine itch, and has nothing to do with money. You can, however, make a career out of being a poet by teaching, traveling around, and giving lectures. It's a thin living at best.

Is it more an avocation than a profession?

I guess that I think of it as a state of the soul. I can't divide it out from anything. It's in the bloodstream.

II
Essays on
Poems, Poets, Poetics

These pieces were for the most part written to order, for inclusion in college textbooks or literary magazines, or, in one instance, as a literary column in a women's magazine of broad circulation. Since they were not conceived as a unit, they touch only tangentially. Here and there they repeat certain convictions. The two articles on Anne Sexton restate fragments that have turned up already in the interviews. I have kept them rather than rupture the fabric of the essay.

On Howard Nemerov's
Journal of the Fictive Life

I am a writer in the margin of books. Emboldened by
solitude, by the absence of teacher or librarian clucking
over my shoulder, I deface the white border with my
bracket marks and exclamations, rejoinders or enthu-
siasms. Years later I often wonder at the heat of my pas-
sion in the margin. Why was I so stirred? Or even: how
could I have been so wrongheaded?

Journals, diaries, letters, and memoirs especially de-
light the voyeur who is the writer in me. I read and am
moved to comment—scrawling sidewise in the margin—on
Katherine Mansfield's tender letters to John Middleton
Murry. Here, D. H. Lawrence regrets an invitation to tea
because Frieda has a bad cold (how democratic the ca-
tarrh!). Virginia Woolf tortures herself over the prospect
of a bad review (the greater the writer, the more suscep-
tible to the critic's bad cess?). Yeats reports that Lady
Gregory is better, but has written to him in pencil that
she very nearly slipped away. (He and I are both appalled
by the "in pencil"; pencil leaves an impermanent smear.)

I think my curiosity about the lives of other writers is

heightened by the fact that I am a woman. I want to see how other women managed their lives, either as the wives of celebrated, memoir-keeping authors, or as writers—wives, mothers?—themselves. Then, too, the relation between person and poet, the pondering of his/her own case, the sharing of the ultimate condition of the writer—that drafty, celestially lonely, often boring condition—draws me to these texts.

A book which has stood the test of my marginalia better than most, a book that agitates and soothes in equal measure, a little-known, undoubtedly undersold book, is *Journal of the Fictive Life*, by Howard Nemerov, published in 1965 by Rutgers University Press. It is an honest, unabashed account of a painfully dry period in the life of a writer. Nemerov seeks to batter his way out of the enclosure by investigating his own creative process, keeping notes during one summer. He details particularly the conflict between the poet and the novelist trapped in his own being, the struggle to let the novelist out. This series of reflections caught and held me fast. *Charming! true!* I have added in the margin alongside: "For a Jewish Puritan of the middle class, the novel is serious, the novel is work, the novel is conscientious application—why, the novel is practically the retail business all over again." Later, *The languor of the first sentence!* stands outside a paragraph on the terror of beginning. "What a great weight one adds to the heart by simply saying, 'It was a fine morning in summer,'" Nemerov has written.

It fascinates, this dichotomy between poet and novelist. Nemerov moves back into his own history, seizes on his dreams, invents others when he cannot drag specifically dreamt ones into the light and attempts to discover, through self-analysis, the sources of his blocks as well as his creativity. *The danger*, I find inked between two paragraphs, *is that the self-analysand tortures his material to fit his scheme*. Other objections are sprinkled in the margins, so that the book in my hand has become a dialogue.

How fitting it seems to reread this book in summer, some twelve years from the season of its actual composition. I am chewing gristle just now to get to the bone of a novel I want to write. *Journal of the Fictive Life* comes through to me this time almost as an exhortation to leave off complaining and begin. "I have tried to keep this inquisition reasonable in tone," Nemerov says toward the end, "certainly not to hoke it up by getting rhapsodic, or by the usual literary claim that all this showed great courage on my part, and therefore must be very grand literature."

Is it too much to claim that home-making women, by virtue of their early encounters with solitude, boredom, and frustration (for instance, three children serially contract chicken pox in November), have an extra modicum of insight into the writer's encounters? Probably. At least I ought to try not to hoke it up. I ought to remember Yeats's disclaimer, in the introduction of his *Essays*, of any connection between the poet and "The bundle of accident and incoherence that sits down to breakfast."

Or, as Nemerov has analyzed the creative process, "No matter how often and how far you digress, no matter how many clever improvisations you make . . . , so long as you keep patiently bringing yourself back."

"Provide, Provide"

I suppose all of us who were born early enough to have one, cherish a personal recollection of Robert Frost. In mine he is quite an old man at the lectern—Sever Hall, I believe—reading his poems with the kind of authority and grace that goes with veneration. It is the era of crew cuts and Veronica Lake hairdos. The cast-iron statesman of poetry has already displayed his best-loved wares and turns now to a less familiar poem, delivering the lines with a hard edge. The last stanza is bitten off and spat out at this collegiate audience. Clearly, he is enjoying himself. Clearly there is lust in his voice as it quavers purposefully on "Provide, provide!"

Age has its own savage pleasures; perhaps chief among them is to admonish the young. There is a stone set in the gateway to an old graveyard that I visit. It avers, with a Frostian accent: "Stop, passengers, as you pass by. / As you are now, so once was I. / As I am now, so you will be. / Prepare for death, and follow me." So is the case made for our mortality and we are properly humbled. In much the same tone, Frost makes the case for expe-

---

"A Note on 'Provide, Provide'" from *Gone Into If Not Explained: Essays on Poems by Robert Frost*, edited by Greg Kuzma, 1976, Best Cellar Press. Reprinted by permission.

diency. As if to say, since no one can be expedient to the point of choosing his own exit from this life, I advise you to get ready, prepare, provide for whatever dreary old age may await you.

I am generally uncomfortable in the presence of the didactic poem, scratching my itches, aware of a hot embarrassment beginning around the ears. The preachy poem is not unlike the pornographic story: however vigorously we deplore both social virtue and private vice, they can rise above their origins to delight us when they work. This poem most purely works. It manifests a Frost far from the Yankee farmer-poet role he has lucklessly been cast in, alternately praised and dismissed for his "easiness"—as easy, say, as Longfellow. "Provide, Provide" is neither optimistic nor orthodox. The lyrics illuminate unsparingly the terrible truth of man's nature. They express an attitude, as Jarrell has said, that "makes pessimism seem a hopeful evasion." For everything will be taken from you in your fall from the fame that passes in our secular world as grace. What little comfort can be salvaged must be bought and paid for in full. But the poem transcends its bleak and stubborn honesty; it ends by delighting or at least gratifying us with its wisdom.

"Like a piece of ice on a hot stove," Frost wrote in a characteristic little dictum, "the poem must ride on its own melting." The poem must come into being, not without discipline and revision certainly, but arrive, a kind of hapless swimmer in the pool of its own sweat, unfolding by surprise, as it were. I would guess that the surprise in the writing of "Provide, Provide" was the way it fell for Frost into triplets. And once the stanza pattern was established, once, as he said, "his wordly commitments [were] now three or four deep," he simply got on with it, got on with the game of working through the meter and line to that brilliant, resonant conclusion.

Notice the word *simply*. It cloaks the whole silent struggle of will that pounds feeling into form, elevates language to match the mood, and makes a straight way through the jungle to a strong closure. "Does anyone," Frost most ingenuously and rhetorically asks, "Does anyone believe I would have committed myself to the treason-reason-season rhyme-set in my 'Reluctance' if I had been blasé enough to know that these three words about exhausted the possibilities?"

It seems to me particularly fitten that "Provide, Provide" should have devolved into this hideously difficult-to-maintain rhyme scheme. To work in rhyming couplets in Anglo-Saxon English, even with recourse to approximate rhymes, taxes the poet and most often tarnishes his charm. To work in threes is to skate close to the open water of light verse. But courting this danger saves the poem from pulpit statement. The multiple rhyme does not banter, but it does swagger a little. The stylistic cut of it lightens the line and intensifies the irony. The felicities of the language prepare us for the consolation prize which is contained in a kind of Yankee glint. Stoicism, dignity, up-country shrewdness. . . . And thus we are prepared for the regional alternate past participle of *buy*. "Boughten friendship" is salvation through necessity, a willed acceptance of the last chaos that life brings. It is not a piety, but a fact, a condition.

Poetry Bound to Delight

It is, quite simply, a joy to sit down with Philip Larkin's twenty-odd new poems collected in *High Windows*, each one eliciting the shiver of recognition that accompanies his flawless exactitude of imagery. The tone in this new book is darker, the poet's voice a shade more ominous, the language perceptibly harsher than before.

But all the old magic of the two earlier books is here. The necromancer continues to work in the most exacting stanzaic patterns; he draws on the most rigorous of rhyme schemes. Yet he never wrenches the normal word order to save a rhyme, nor does he lose the easy conversational flow made memorable, say, in "Toads" (from *The Less Deceived*):

> Lots of folks live up lanes
> With fires in a bucket,
> Eat windfalls and tinned sardines—
> They seem to like it.
>
> Their nippers have got bare feet,
> Their unspeakable wives
> Are skinny as whippets—and yet
> No one actually *starves*.

Reprinted by permission of the *Boston Globe*. First appeared January 5, 1975.

Poverty precisely nailed, despair made measurable and memorable, a kind of limping, British-style stoicism in the face of decay, all are underscored by Larkin's ironic tone.

How metrically easy he makes it sound, returning to this theme in "Toads Revisited" (from *The Whitsun Weddings*):

> What else can I answer,
> When the lights come on at four
> At the end of another year?
> Give me your arm, old toad;
> Help me down Cemetery Road.

With skills like these—form married to a relentless registry of the senses—Larkin might well be charged with the dreaded epithet, poet's poet. What saves him is that he is never caught with his technique showing. He does not trot out literary allusions nor make a display of his erudition, but his fine intelligence, now sharpened by the cutting edge of middle age, is at work.

Loneliness is here, and old age. Sex, groped for and consummated. Mothers and fathers. Grubbing for a living. The occasional moment of nobility inside the commonplace.

The brilliant, hard, specific detail that clinches the poem is Larkin's hallmark. In a bittersweet, grudging lyric about new life-styles and easy sex, the image he develops and turns, from the heedlessness of youth to the foreboding of age, is that of "going down the long slide." The visual suggestion of a playground slide down which life inexorably shoots in the one preordained direction then opens out at the end of the poem into the surprise of the image "high windows." Sunlight, blue sky, broad vistas for this poet mean infinite loss and infinite solitude. It is a beautiful despair rather than simply a bleak one.

A magnificent, and by Larkin's standard, long poem on old age, moves from "Perhaps being old is having lighted rooms / Inside your head, and people in them, acting" to the final metaphor of death as "extinction's alp." It is "the peak that stays in view wherever we go"; an unexpected image, this is surely an unforgettable one.

Larkin takes a passionate attitude toward the oblivion he particularizes, and the illumination cast by these poems is almost eerily bright. This is a book to cherish.

Reminiscence Delivered at
Memorial Service for Anne Sexton
in Marsh Chapel, Boston University

October 15, 1974

Yesterday at my desk, trying to sort out a few things to say here, I spent hours going through folders of old letters, work sheets, scraps of poems. For one thing, I was trying to pinpoint what year it was—1956? 1957?—that Anne and I met, two shy housewives, a pair of closet poets, in John Holmes's class at the Boston Center for Adult Education. For another, I was trying to sort out people's names, who and where we were, how Sam Albert was in that class, and Ruth Soter, the friend to whom "With Mercy for the Greedy" is dedicated, and how we first met George Starbuck when he read at the New England Poetry Club in 1958.

Most of this I gleaned from Holmes's letters, traveling from Medford to Newton, from 1957 to a month before his death in 1962, letters written between our workshop meetings, or because of them, or even in spite of them. George's name comes up frequently, and Sam Albert's name, and specific poems we are working on get mentioned. The group came down hard on Anne's poem, "Housewife," and she revised it well. Anne read the poem "For Eleanor Boylan Talking with God" at a workshop and it was enthusiastically received, except for some pruning needed at the end. There was no more determined reviser than Anne. She worried and snipped and pounded the ending into its final, poignant form.

Remembering this, the whole complex rich interplay of workshop comes back, of Holmes and Starbuck and Albert and Sexton and Kumin during the three years we held forth on our own over coffee and whiskey and carbon copies of our poems, and before that, around the long oak table at 5 Commonwealth Avenue in a second-story room that smelled of chalk and wet overshoes. There, Anne and I, in a funny mixture of timidity and bravado, prayed that our poems would rise to the top of the pile under Professor Holmes's fingers as he alternately fussed with his pipe and shuffled pages, and one of us would thus be divinely elected for scrutiny.

Later, for one semester, there were Ted and Renee Weiss, Ted a visiting professor at MIT. Anne had just written "Woman with Girdle." The poem's mischief roused Ted to such heights of ribaldry that night and we were all so raucous that the couple overhead—this was at Weiss's borrowed apartment somewhere in Cambridge—thumped on the floor and threatened us with the police and we were, to our shame, even noisier. That same winter John Crowe Ransom came to Tufts at Holmes's invitation and Anne and I drove to Medford in a blizzard to hear him. Somehow we drove back again too, at three o'clock in the morning, straddling the yellow line that divided a deserted and snow-clogged highway. We were sleepy and exalted and a little drunk on bourbon and fish chowder and the marvelous voice of the poet saying his own best lines.

I found an old poem of John's about another, earlier workshop that lasted through three winters in the forties, a workshop consisting of Ciardi, Wilbur, Eberhart, May Sarton, and John Holmes. It says what we were, too, and why, and now I'd like to close with these few lines from it:

Good God bless all such big long bickering nights
Among the cheeses and bottles, coffee and carbon copies,
In Medford or Cambridge—or Nashville or Chicago!
The fact is that everything we read is in our books,
Our best poems. If those confrontations were painful,
Rowdy, sometimes the bloom of fire and absolute,
We couldn't hear a clank of armor some of us wore,
Or see which came naked and afraid, but it was so.

Look at us now, in the long story's foreseeable ending,
Such a yardage of books on shelves . . .
We remind one another, when we meet now, of those nights,
How we had what we remember, the warmth of the poems.

Sexton's *The Awful Rowing Toward God*

The poems in *The Awful Rowing Toward God* were written during a crisis time in Anne Sexton's life, a period of great personal anguish and at the same time of intense, even manic creativity. There is no psychic distance between the poet and the poem; on the contrary, the poem is an almost tangible physical extension of the psyche, a kind of third hand or eye. Robert Motherwell said, in an essay on art, "there is a certain point on the curve of anguish where one encounters the comic." So it is in these poems. They are all signed with her vivid imagery. Again and again we are tossed on the curve, saved, refreshed, by the satire, the self-mock, the comic inner lining of the macabre. Reticence forms no part of Sexton's style, nor economy, nor brusque reason. The poem is a defense against isolation, against memories so terrible that they erode the senses to the edge of hallucination.

We were for eighteen years warm personal friends. During the late winter of 1973, while these poems were being constructed out of blood and sorrow and fury, I was living in Kentucky as writer-in-residence at Centre College. We had agreed before I left Boston to divide the

First appeared in the *American Poetry Review* 4, no. 3 (May-June, 1975). Reprinted by permission.

long-distance telephone bill; further, we had agreed to talk on the reduced-rate side of the ledger, after five P.M. or before eight A.M. My rooms in Danville abutted a Baptist church with a dependable clock that pinged on the quarters and tolled the hours. And every afternoon at five, a concert of Baptist hymns. But just as the carillons embarked on their opening measure, the ringing of my phone would float up through those other bells, and we would talk across the early dark of a Boston winter into the twilight of a bluegrass one. For the most part, we dispensed with amenities of time and place quickly and got down to the professional business of the poems— mostly hers, for she was writing with the urgency of a fugitive one length ahead of the posse. As indeed she was.

One other fact. As is evident from her poetry, Anne Sexton was strongly attracted to, indeed sought vigorously a kind of absolutism in religion that was missing from the Protestantism of her inheritance. She wanted God as a sure thing, an Old Testament avenger admonishing his Chosen People, an authoritarian yet forgiving God decked out in sacrament and ceremony. Judaism and Catholicism each exerted a strong gravitational pull. Divine election, confession and absolution, the last rites, these were her longings. And then an elderly, sympathetic priest, one of many priests she encountered— accosted might be a better word—along the way, said a saving thing to her, said the magic and simple fact that kept her alive at least a year beyond her time, and made the awful rowing a possibility. "God is in your typewriter," he told her. Thus she went to her typewriter and thus, according to your lights, she found, or invented Him.

A Friendship Remembered

As the world knows, we were intimate friends and professional allies. Early on in our friendship, indeed almost as soon as we began to share poems, we began to share them on the telephone. Since we lived initially in the same Boston suburb and later in contiguous ones (Ma Bell's unlimited contiguous service be praised!), there were no message units to reckon with, which surely would have inhibited me, though probably not Annie, whose long-distance phone bills were monumental down the years. It was her habit, when alone at night (and alone at night meant depressed always, sometimes anxious to the point of pain as well) to call on old friends. But that's a digression. What I wanted to say was I don't know what year, but fairly early on, we both installed second phone lines in our houses so that the rest of each of our families—the two husbands, the five children— could have equal access to a phone and we could talk privately for as long as we wanted. I confess we sometimes connected with a phone call and kept that line linked for hours at a stretch, interrupting poem-talk to

"A Friendship Remembered" by Maxine Kumin from *Anne Sexton: The Artist and Her Critics*, edited by J. D. McClatchy. (Bloomington: Indiana University Press, 1978). Reprinted by permission.

stir the spaghetti sauce, switch the laundry, or try out a new image on the typewriter; we whistled into the receiver for each other when we were ready to resume. It worked wonders. And to think that it only cost seven or eight bucks a month!

How different from January and February of 1973, when I went to Centre College in Danville, Kentucky, as a writer-in-residence. We agreed ahead of time to divide the phone bill we would incur. Anne called me every afternoon at five; she was then writing *The Awful Rowing Toward God* at white heat—two, three, even four poems a day. I tried hard to retard the process for I felt it was all happening too fast and it scared me. It was too much like Plath spewing out those last poems. Nevertheless, I listened, commented, helped, tried to provide some sort of organizational focus. We averaged one hour a day on the phone, only because I was too cheap to talk longer. My share of the bill came to about three hundred dollars, which was pretty liberated for me. I am descended from a lineage that panics as soon as the three-minute mark is passed.

Writing poems and bouncing them off each other by phone does develop the ear. You learn to hear line breaks, to pick up and be critical of unintended internal rhyme, or intended slant rhyme or whatever. We did this so comfortably and over such an extended period of time that indeed when we met—usually over lunch at my house, for Anne almost always stopped off to lunch with me after seeing whichever of her infamously inept psychiatrists—we were somewhat shy of each other's poem there on the page. I can remember so often saying, "oh, so *that's* what it looks like" of a poem I had heard and visualized through half a dozen revisions.

Over the years, her lines shortened and the line breaks grew, I think, more unexpected. In the early days we were both working quite strictly in form. We measured and cut and pasted and reworked arduously, with an intense sense of purpose, both of us believing in the rigors of form as a forcing agent, that the hardest truths would come right if they were hammered to fit (see the title poem in *All My Pretty Ones*). I confess we both had rhyming dictionaries and we both used them. Typically, we had totally different kinds. Anne's grouped rhyme-words according to their common endings—all the one-syllable words, for example, followed by the two-syllable ones, and so on—whereas mine worked by orthography, which made it quirkier because it went not by sound but by spelling. It was Anne's aim to use rhyme unexpectedly, brilliantly but aptly. Even the most unusual rhyme, she felt, must never obtrude on the sense of the line, nor must the normal word order, the easy tone of natural vernacular usuage, be wrenched to save a rhyme. She would willingly push a poem through twenty or more drafts; she had an unparalleled tenacity and only abandoned a "failed" poem with regret if not downright anger after dozens of sessions.

Nevertheless, I would say that Anne's poems were frequently "given" ones. "Riding the Elevator into the Sky" (in *The Awful Rowing Toward God*) is an example. The newspaper article mentioned in its first stanza gave rise to the poem and the poem itself came quite easily and cleanly, as if written out beforehand in the clear air and then transcribed onto the page with very few alterations. "Letter Written on a Ferry while Crossing Long Island Sound" (in *All My Pretty Ones*) was a "given" poem, too; given by the fortuitous sight of the nuns. As I remember it, the poem was written much as it now appears on the printed page, except for the minor skirmishes required to effect that marvelous closure in each stanza where the fourth from the last and the last lines rhyme (save for the first stanza, and "cup" and "up" in the middle of the last stanza). Also, it was orginally called "Letter Written on the Long Island Ferry" and was was made more specific on the advice of Howard Moss. "Young" and "I Remember" (both also in *All My Pretty Ones*) required very little revision, as my memory serves, whereas "The Truth the Dead Know" went through innumerable workings to arrive at its final form. In this poem, the poet is locked into an *a b a b* rhyme scheme with little room for pyrotechnics. The language is purified to an amazing degree, I think, reflecting Anne's wish to open *All My Pretty Ones* with a spare, terse, tough elegy for her parents, one without biographical detail, the very detail she would get into later, in the title poem or in "The House." That title poem was one which underwent many revisions to force it into the exigency of an *abab cdcd ee* stanza. We both admired the multisyllabic rhymes of "slumber" / "disencumber" and "navigator" / "later", to say nothing of the *tour de force* final couplet.

The initial impetus for her poems usually came as a direct visitation to the cave of her desk. She invoked the muse by reading other poets and playing her favorite records over and over. The background of music acted in some way to free her to create, which always astonished me, for whom it is an intrusion. Often with the volume turned up loud, loud enough to drown out all other sounds, she could pull an intricate rhyme scheme out of the air. Is it worth noting that massed orchestral strings, full volume, served too as a device for her to cover and block out the bad voices? (The time before the time she killed herself, it was with music at crescendo: a scream, I thought when I got there. I don't know if the radio was playing that last time; I think so.) As for her subject matter, we all know it came for the most part directly out of her own life and times, with little if any psychic distance on the trauma or pleasure that gave rise to the poem. Still, she transmuted the events. She was able to take the rawest facts—her mother's agonizingly slow death from cancer, her father's stroke, her entire wretched childhood experience as what was undoubtedly an undiagnosed hyperkinetic youngster, kept behind a gate in her own room—and to make of them a whole.

Someone once said that we have art in order not to die of the truth. Sexton's confessional poems most vividly and truly not only kept her alive, but they sustained and spoke to a vast audience. I would say that she drew great sustenance and comfort from the knowledge that her work reached out to and beyond the normal sensitive reader of poetry (though, for God's sake, what is "normal" or "sensitive"?) and touched the minds of many deeply troubled people. For a while it seemed that psychiatrists all over the country were referring their patients to Anne's work, as if it were the balm in Gilead. At the same time that it comforted and fed her to know that she mattered as a poet beyond the usual sphere of self-congratulating, self-adulating bards, she had considerable ambivalence about her work. Accused of exhibitionism, she was determined only to be more flamboyant; nevertheless, the large Puritan hiding inside suffered and grieved over the label "confessional" poet. For instance, when she wrote "Cripples and Other Stories" (in *Live or Die*), a poem that almost totally "occurred" on the page, she crumpled it up, as if in embarrassment, and tossed it into the wastebasket. We fished it out and saved it; I thought it then and think it now a remarkable document.

The "saving" of that poem was to make the tone consistent and to smooth out some of the cruder rhythmical spots. This was the sort of mechanical task Anne could fling herself into gladly. The results were often doubly effective. In "The Operation" (a key poem in *All My Pretty Ones*), for example, the experience—awesome and painful—is hammered into art by way of form and rhyme. Both squeeze the raw event until the juice runs in the reader, I think. I do not mean to downplay the force of metaphor in the poem—the "historic thief," the "Humpty-Dumpty," etc.—but it is the impact of rhyme and the shape of the poem's three parts (i.e., its form) that bring it off. For instance, the retardation of the rhyming sounds at the end of the first section—"leaf" / "straw" / "lawn" / "car" / "thief" / "house" / "upon"— in those short, fairly sharply end-stopped lines, build to the impact. Or, to take yet another poem, I remember "Faustus and I" (in *The Death Notebooks*) was headed for the discard pile; it was then a free-verse poem and as such had, for me, an evilly flippant tone. I seem to remember that I often helplessly suggested, "why don't you pound it into form?" and often it worked. In the case of "Faustus and I" the suggestion worked because the rhyme scheme gave the poem a dignity and nobility it deserved. It worked because the pounding elicited a level of language, a level of metaphor, she hadn't quite reached in the early versions.

Anne also had an almost mystical faith in the "found" word or image, as well as in metaphor by mistake, by typo or misapprehension. She would fight hard to keep an image, a line, a word usage, but if you were just as dogged in your conviction that the line didn't work, was sentimental or mawkish, that the word usage was ill suited or trite, she would capitulate—unless she was totally convinced of her own rightness. Then there was no shaking her. We learned somehow, from each other and from trusting each other's critical sense, not to go past the unshakable core, not to trespass on style or voice.

Perhaps we learned this in the early years of our student workshops, first at the Boston Center in classes with John Holmes, and later in our own house by house workshops with John Holmes and George Starbuck and Sam Albert. These were often real encounters, real square-offs, but we all respected and admired one another—an idea that seems terribly old-fashioned somehow today, that poets could be competitive and full of ego but genuinely care for one another's well-being. That was a good group, now that I think back on it; we all wrote at white heat and many of the best poems any of us ever wrote were tested in that crucible. Anne, in fact, as a result of this experience, came to believe in the value of workshops. She loved growing this way herself, and she urged the technique on her students. Her whole *Bedlam* book grew during her workshop years and virtually every one of those poems was scrutinized across the table. We were still at it when *All My Pretty Ones* was in process. It was awesome the way Anne could come to the workshop biweekly with three, four, five new and complicated poems. She was never meek about it, but she did listen and she did care. She gave generous help and she required, demanded, insisted on generous response.

We might talk for a moment about *Transformations*. Anne was fascinated by fairy tales. They were for her what the Greek myths had been, perhaps, for others. Since she had not had—and she was grim about this—the advantage of a higher education (by which she meant Beowulf, the Norse eddas, Homer, Milton, etc.—all denied her), she lapsed back to what must have been a halcyon time in her life, the time when her great aunt, the colossal mother figure of her past, had read German fairy tales to her. Now she reread them all and scoured the libraries for more, even asking my daughter Judy to translate and retranslate some tales from the German so that she could be sure she had gotten every final variant on the story. The wonderful self-mocking, society-mocking wit of *Tranformations* is entirely her own; she was a very funny person, quick to satirize a given situation. The book more or less evolved; she had no thought of a collection at first, and I must immodestly state that I urged and bullied her to go on after the first few poems to think in terms of a whole book of them. I also take outright credit for the title. We had been talking about the way many contemporary poets translated from languages they did not themselves read, but used trots or had the poems filtered through an interpreter, and that' these poems were *adaptations*. It struck me then that Anne's poems about the fairy tales went one step further and were *transformations*. And for the record let me state that in that same conversation Annie was urging me to collect the "pastoral" poems I'd written, and I said, "but what will I call it?" and she said, "*Up Country*, of course."

The Book of Folly gives further evidence of Anne's interest in myth making. Whether or not they succeed, she has written three myths of her own and she labored strenuously in the vineyard of prose, finding it foreign and harsh work. But it is true that the storyteller inside the poet sometimes yearns desperately to be let out. Anne's storyteller burst out in these tales, and in the Daisy play she wrote early in her career on a Ford grant. (*Tell Me Your Answer True* was its original title, though it ended up as *Mercy Street*—an image that turned up in a dream, the dream a plea for mercy from somewhere, anywhere, from Life.) It wasn't the first verbalization of her Christ fascination, nor was it destined to be the last. Christ as Prime Sufferer, and God (any kind of god who'd be there) became her final obsessions, perhaps because as her life deteriorated, people were less dependable. But Jesus figured prominently from the very beginning.

What I chiefly remember is how much fun Anne had working on the play, how richly she enjoyed working in dialogue, for which she had a considerable talent. Her ear was quick and true; I always trusted implicitly her criticism of the dialogue in my fiction, and could point to dozens of lines—responses, usually—in my own work which came pure out of Sexton's mouth. She also loved the excitement of being in the theater and being in New York and staying at the Algonquin. She adored her leading actress Marian Seldes (as who would not!), and loved most of all the late late nights after a rehearsal when she would sit up till dawn reworking a speech here, a phrase there, loving the tinkering even more than the glamor of actually having her play produced.

Anne's way of working, whether with a poem or the play or an attempted story, was to try out the draft on as many listeners as she could amass. I felt sometimes that she was putting the matter to a vote, and indeed in her classes at Boston University she fell into the always amusing pattern of inviting the students to vote for or against an image, a line break, an ending. But she invited and need the interchange of ideas and attitudes, something that is anathema to most writers, who cannot brook outside interference or involvement in an unfinished piece. Anne took strength from outside reactions, as much strength from the negative as from the positive remarks (I am not now speaking of reviewers!), and genuinely felt that there was always something to be gained in this sharing process. It was her conviction that the least experienced student could bring something to bear on a work sheet; she weighed and evaluated opinions, keeping some, discarding others, but using them all as a kind of emotional ballast for going on with her work.

And she was equally willing to bring her own energy to bear on the meanest poem. She was generous, yes; but it transcends generosity, really. It was evangelical, it was for Poetry, the Higher Good. She lived her poetry, poetry was her life. It had saved her life in a real sense when, in the mid-1950s she began to write poems as a therapeutic act urged on her by her then psychiatrist. The clear thread that runs through all the books of poems is how tenuous that life was. She was on loan to poetry, as it were. We always knew it would end. We just didn't know when or exactly how.

The Making of "Mother Rosarine"

> When Mother Rosarine died,
> I was late for the funeral.

So begins the work sheet of the finished poem printed at the end of this article. It was a poem that hung back, resisting all my efforts to bring it into form and coherence, for most of one March and April a few years ago.

Today, thumbing through the thick accumulation of yellow pages, each one numbered and dated out of some stubborn conviction I clung to that the puzzle would solve itself and the poem be made, I have mixed feelings of pleasure and frustration.

Pleasure at how much of the essence of the final draft is contained on that first work sheet—I try to make a mental note to trust my first chaotic instincts in such matters from now on.

Frustration at how many blind alleys I entered and then had to back out of as I followed the maze day after day that led to the center.

I remember the genesis of the urge to write this particular poem. I had been visiting my home town in

Pennsylvania. At some point in the course of a casual conversation in the way that you catch up on local history when you've been absent a long time, my mother said to me, "Did you know that Mother Rosarine died?"

"No! When?"

"This winter. I thought I wrote and told you. She'd been sick a long time. It was a blessing, really."

It wasn't a shocking fact in distance or in time. Mother Rosarine had served as the Mother Superior of the Convent of the Sisters of Saint Joseph. Through all the years of my childhood and adolescence, she and her nuns had been our next-door neighbors.

Side by side we were Catholics and Jews in a predominantly Protestant suburb. I ranged as freely through the nunnery as other youngsters might swarm in a park or playground. I had always thought of it as my second home. As the poem progressed, it began to seem as though the convent had been perhaps my first home.

"Lying last night on borrowed sheets," I wrote, "I dreamed back my nuns in a jangling mansion." I had no idea I was finding the key to the poem when the rhyme came: "they mooed like cows in their stanchions, making the sound of prayer."

The notion of borrowed sheets persisted. Where did I think I belonged? So did the concept of putting it all in a dream.

Soon I was "dragging behind me down the impersonal street my ragbag memories," again and again recreating in lines that didn't quite match but were seeking out rhymes that early and sweet memory of the sisters at prayer.

One association triggered another. Invented or real? Does it matter? There was a day of trying to write in the deaths of my grandparents, the Jewish custom of covering the mirrors with sheets. There was a day of reviewing the nuns' infrequent visits to my own house, once on the occasion of my brother's nearly fatal illness. They came to pray for him.

"Mother came with her littlest nuns, Sister Marie Theresa and Sister Serena Catherine—her best basketball players."

None of it worked. Worse than that, it was terrible prosy stuff. But the basketball games! I had forgotten the basketball games, and all those wrong turns had led me back to them.

Finally, a fresh start one morning: "Mother, Mother Rosarine, sharp white front and black feathers." Direct description. It seemed that the poem would begin.

"Mother Mother" continued to haunt me for pages as the first stanza took shape and a rhyme scheme emerged. It was a loose pattern, relying on slant or approximate rhymes as much as on strict on-rhymes.

From the first clicking together of "mansion-stanchion," rhyme sounds involving two syllables, there evolved other feminine endings: "linens," "kingdom," and so on. I had a hard time getting rid of "feathers." It was too birdlike. I toyed with "vest," "stem," "bosom" and "habit" before "buckram" arrived. Finally, "Mother Mother" gave way to "Next-door Mother." It was clear where I belonged, and I was on my way.

Scribbled in ink on the next sheet is a message to myself: "Saint Theresa—no use trying to be angels. Look up!" it says. Three pages further on, I must have done so, although by then I had reverted to the idea of using a dream and had written: "In that murdering dream, a delegation came down for their queen."

Immediately after, a quotation from the life of Teresa of Avila: "We are not angels but have bodies, and it is madness for us to want to become angels while we are still on earth."

Whatever the link was, it led me, on the next page, to: "and I woke, hot in my body still." This was followed by: "made wrong born wrong for the convent school." There was nothing else on that page, an indication that a day had passed.

More blind starts and more dead ends, but the first two stanzas were now quite firm. Two pages further on, another message to myself, this one in pencil and followed by a phone number and part of a grocery list, says: "I remember she said rooting for your side is a useful passion."

But I went off the track again. "Lying in terror on muslin sheets / I dreamed her heart in that quilted mansion / signed out sadly, but found it sweet." Then some gibberish ending with "sneakered feet." I was still caught in the dream, although the sheets I was sleeping on at least were no longer borrowed.

At that point, I desperately returned to the first two stanzas and simply retyped them, here and there switching a word to correct the meter or grammar. I pretended that that was enough.

On the third round, the mechanical act of striking the keys took over and the rhythm of the poem swung me into: "Wrong, born wrong for the convent games / I hunched on the sidelines, beggar fashion." My penciled note flew in effortlessly, and I went on. Hooray for the basketball games! "My child, said Mother Rosarine, rooting for your side is a useful passion." The rest of that stanza was easy.

Promptly the next day, the real or imagined incident of stealing the rosary beads arose. It had been lurking around for quite a while, ever since the idea of "boarders" came up in the first stanza. There were notations that said "day-girls," "boarders," "living in."

Now that I had come far enough in the poem to recognize myself as the outsider, I was able to use the connecting link that the quotation from Saint Theresa had evoked, for I was no angel and had indeed a body still.

The fourth stanza thus began, "At vespers, hot in my body still." And then the confession of the theft. It must have seemed to me as a child an offense of enormous magnitude, and perhaps that is why it took so long to surface. Possibly it never happened; possibly it was just a theatrical invention. But for the sake of the poem I was glad to have it.

The rest was all downhill, for I had almost written the ending before the poem properly began. Obviously the nuns had represented for me a terribly safe, highly idealized, asexual, and direct route to the kingdom of heaven.

Mother Rosarine had been a second or surrogate mother, a good harbor from whatever small storms were then ruffling my private life. I had begun thinking to write an elegy. I had ended with a poem in praise.

MOTHER ROSARINE

Next-door Mother Rosarine
Of the square white front and black buckram
Tugged up the morning with cinches of keys,
Rode through The Mass, a bristle-chinned queen,
Jingling the tongues that unlocked the linens,
The larder, the gym suits that luffed at the knees
Of the boarders, and swung on the door to His Kingdom

Through which I did not dare pass.
I came in screw curls and dotted swisses,
Came through the hedge to that swaddled lap.
Cheeks on her starch, a traitor to my class,
I nibbled Christ's toes on the rosewood cross
And begged her, Mother, take off your cap.
Oh I filled up my vestal with baby kisses.

Wrong, born wrong for the convent games
I hunched on the sidelines, beggar fashion.
My child, said Mother Rosarine,
Rooting for your side is a useful passion.
She led three cheers and a locomotive for the team.
Beet-red Sister Mary Claire, a victim
Of rashes, refereed. She called for time.

At vespers, hot in my body still,
I stole back in up the convent stairs
And sat alone with the varnished smell
Of the scribbled desks, and dreamed of angels.
There were lids to pry in the chalkdust air.
A rosary strung with lacquer-black kernels
Slid in my pocket. It polished my fingers.

The seeds grew wet in my palm. Going down,
Clicking the blessings I made my own
And testing the treads for creaks, I could hear
Mother Rosarine's voice turn the churn downstairs.
In the buttery sunset, in the beadroll mansion,
Her nuns, like rows of cows in their stanchions
Softly mooing, were making the sound of prayer.

A Questionnaire

The questionnaire and checklist referred to in the following piece contain such questions as: "How did the poem start?" "What changes did it go through from start to finish?" "What principles of technique did you consciously use?" "How many drafts did the poem go through?" "What rhythmical principles did you use?" and so on. I find I am not offended by this sort of inquiry; I think it is a useful tool, particularly for the beginning poet or student of contemporary poetry. Almost everyone invited to respond to the questionnaire did so. Some prepared lengthy essays on their individual *ars poetica*. But here and there a dissenting voice: "This is disgusting." Another: "As a poet my primary concern is not with the facilitation of understanding." All of which merely supports my notion that while poets, like politicians, range across the spectrum, the poem, like the cheese in "Old MacDonald Had a Farm," stands alone.

I will try just impressionistically now to talk about how

"How It Goes On" by Maxine Kumin, reprinted from *Fifty Contemporary Poets: The Creative Process*, edited by Alberta T. Turner. Copyright © 1977 by Longman, Inc. By permission of Longman and the author.

"How It Goes On" got written, with one eye on the questionnaire and one eye on the checklist.

The poem was initiated by a fact: I had a pair of lambs (Southdown ewes, named Gertrude Stein and Alice B. Toklas), and the older one strangled to death in a freak accident, leaving this one to be disposed of somehow before the winter snow. Up until the very last work sheet the poem was called "The Lambs." This was the theme, but the simple narrative did not seem to be enough to sustain the poem, nor indeed suit my very dark and depressed mood of those winter months. Thus the poem began—it was to be a poem of lambs, of going off to slaughter, and I had intended to make a parallel with the suicide of a close friend. I couldn't do it. It didn't work; the two sets of facts refused to intersect in a sensible way and eventually I discarded everything but the first two stanzas and the ending and put the poem away.

I don't remember how long after, but certainly several weeks, I picked up the work sheets again and began fiddling—you might call it free associating—and what came back into my consciousness was the terrible memory of the slaughter of the wild horses in Idaho. I suppose you might say that for me animals in general and horses in particular represent a kind of lost innocence in our technological society and they often stand as a symbol for mute suffering. And little by little the other details arrived and were fitted together to prepare for the ending, those last two stanzas, which I had had from the very beginning. As is so often the case, the ending seemed quite clear to me before the poem was properly begun.

The poem went through about twenty drafts, if you can call each addition and subtraction on a fresh piece of paper a draft. There's always a lot of material that doesn't fit in and has to be pulled out of the poem. I don't think I ever consciously use anything that can be called a principle of technique. It is hard to answer a lot of the items on the checklist because these items seem to me to presuppose a much more conscious process of creation than I am aware of. Indeed, I am afraid to inquire too closely because I don't want to meddle with whatever it is that happens, whatever it is the muse brings forth. Obviously, though, I rely heavily on free association, trying to let everything come that will come and then building around selected items. In the drafts I would say that the poem expanded rather than shrank, the structure stayed quite constant—an informal kind of long rhyming narrative stanza—theme and tone remained constant and practically everything in the first two stanzas as well as the last six lines came through every rewrite almost unscathed. The changes that took place were not so much in the areas you list, but were changes in substance and in direction.

My line breaks are pretty simpleminded. I end-stop fairly strongly and I lean on rhyme when it is feasible, rhyme including a lot of slant or off variations. The rhythm is largely iambic, as I think befits this sort of conversational tone of voice, or melancholy disquisition on the state of things.

As far as sound repetition goes, I don't have any principles. I try to stay away from heavy alliteration and other pyrotechnics because I think they detract from the sense of the poem and blur the imagery.

I would prefer this poem to be read aloud. Never to musical accompaniment.

On metaphor: well, metaphor is the language of poetry, it is the informing thrust of the language and practically everything is a metaphor, while at the same time pretending to be simple everyday speech. I am quite conscious of this and want all of my literal statements of detail to intensify metaphorically when I can.

As for abstract language, etc., you might say damn tootin I try at all costs to avoid. I hate them.

Nothing conscious about sentence structure.

As for reference and allusion, I am leery of literary allusions unless they are pretty readily accessible—biblical, say, or mythic—as I dislike esoterica in poetry. I would especially want to stay away from private allusive stuff directed at fellow poets, I avoid poems that are about the poetic process for the most part, even though they are very tempting to write.

As for principles of structure, I guess I almost invariably follow a sort of psychological order as in dreams or free association.

And I invariably look for a fairly conclusive ending. My pet peeve is the poem that leaves me turning the page in search of its ending—only to discover it *has* ended.

The persona is me. Why not?

I do try to stay far from cliché unless there is a way to shave it.

To appeal to the reader's eye, I like to make stanza breaks that leave a little white on the page; if a poem is all in a block, one hesitates to read it.

The tone of this poem is deliberate, reflective, brooding.

Yes, it can be paraphrased, by anybody. I don't think it's very different from my other work unless it is a little darker in tone. I don't think poets can consciously help what they write or what tone they take. I don't visualize any particular reader, I just hope the perfect audience of one is out there somewhere and I don't write for anyone in particular. In fact, I don't even write because I want to, but more because I have to.

How It Goes On

Today I trade my last unwise
ewe lamb, the one who won't leave home,
for two cords of stove-length oak
and wait on the old enclosed
front porch to make the swap.
November sun revives the thick
trapped buzz of horseflies. The siren
for noon and forest fires blows
a sliding scale. The lamb of woe
looks in at me through glass
on the last day of her life.

Geranium scraps from the window box
trail from her mouth, burdock burrs
are stickered to her fleece like chicken pox,
under her tail stub, permanent smears.

I think of how it goes on,
this dark particular bent of our hungers:
the way wire eats into a tree
year after year on the pasture's perimeter,
keeping the milk cows penned
until they grow too old to freshen;
of how the last wild horses were scoured
from canyons in Idaho, roped, thrown,
their nostrils twisted shut with wire
to keep them down, the mares aborting,
days later, all of them carted to town.

I think of how it will be
in January, nights so cold
the pond ice cracks like target practice,
daylight glue-colored, sleet falling,
my yellow horse slick with the ball-bearing
sleet, raising up from his dingy browse
out of boredom and habit
to strip bark from the fenced-in trees;
of February, month of the hard palate,
the split wood running out,
worms working in the flour bin.

The lamb, whose time has come, goes off
in the cab of the dump truck, tied to the seat
with baling twine, durable enough
to bear her to the knife and rafter.

O lambs! The whole wolf-world sits down to eat
and cleans its muzzle after.

Kumin on Kumin

The Tribal Poems

A terrible ego, as rife among poets as roundworm in the barnyard, had caused all of us represented in this collection of essays by women writers to agree to examine critically some aspect of our own work. Some will argue that we leap to do so because we are women and only recently in the history of American letters has the woman writer been taken seriously. Since I began as a poet in the Dark Ages of the fifties with very little sense of who I was—a wife, a daughter, a mother, a college instructor, a swimmer, a horse lover, a hermit—a stewpot of conflicting emotions has given me some sympathy with that point of view.

But I suspect that the desire to be heard is purer, or more purely corrupt than that. Every poet everywhere longs to be understood, to plead his/her case before the tribunal. To explicate an image, to verify an attitude, to point out the intricacies of a rhyme scheme or stanzaic pattern is a far brighter fate than to take up a soap box in Hyde Park. And although I have not been unhappy

---

Written while at Princeton, 1977. The collected essays have not yet been published.

with the epithet "pastoral" which is routinely applied to my work, although I do not deny that I write a poetry concerned with the smallest particulars in the natural world, I too have a thesis to advance.

I would like to discuss here in chronological order certain of my "tribal poems"—poems of kinship and parenting—that span two decades. Three of them are taken from *Halfway*, my first collection, long since out of print. They were written in the late fifties; it was not popular then to speak of the uterus or the birth canal. The Women's Movement was still unfounded. An editor of a national magazine wrote me with regret that he could not accept any more poems from me for six months or so because he had already published a woman poet the preceding month.

But what interests me about these poems now is not so much the sociology of the situation to which I was stupidly inured. I am more interested in reading the poet's opening statement of what is to be for her a recurring theme: the separation, for the sake of identity, of mother from child and child from the parental milieu, and her changing perceptions of that separation.

Indeed, I am going to speak of myself henceforth as "the poet" in hopes that the third person usage will cleanse memory and provide objectivity.

Nightmare

This dwelt in me who does not know me now,
Where in her labyrinth I cannot follow,
Advance to be recognized, displace her terror;
I hold my heartbeat on my lap and cannot comfort her.
Tonight she is condemned to cry out wolf
Or werewolf, and it echoes in the gulf
And no one comes to cradle cold Narcissus;
The first cell that divided separates us.

Eight lines, predominantly iambic pentameter, except for the longer fourth line which stands as the fulcrum of the poem, a poem rhyming in slant couplets. Two mythic allusions, one old English, the other classical Greek, neither of them difficult. These are the tools the poet uses to deal with strongly felt or painfully perceived material. She liked then, she likes to this day to cram hard thoughts into formal patterns, thereby rendering them malleable or at least bearable. It became her conviction over the years that form can provide a staunch skeleton on which to set the flesh and blood of feeling. Moreover, she came to believe that the exigencies of rhyme force her to a heightened level of language, especially of metaphor. A level she might not rise to on her own, so to speak. These, then, are her shibboleths.

"The first cell that divided separates us." The child must grow according to her own clock. The parent must make the effort of consent, must relinquish her offspring. If not gracefully, then a great ragged tearing will ensue.

The Journey
for Jane at thirteen

Papers in order; your face
accurate and on guard in the cardboard house
and the difficult patois you will speak
half mastered in your jaw;
the funny make-up in your funny pocketbook—
pale lipstick, half a dozen lotions
to save your cloudless skin
in that uncertain sea
where no one charts the laws—
of course you do not belong to me
nor I to you
and everything is only true in mirrors.

I help to lock your baggage:
history book, lace collar and pink pearls

from the five-and-ten,
an expurgated text
of how the gods behaved on Mount Olympus,
and pennies in your shoes.
You lean as bland as sunshine on the rails.
Whatever's next—
the old oncoming uses
of your new troughs and swells—
is coin for trading among girls
in gym suits and geometry classes.

How can you know I traveled here,
stunned, like you, by my reflection
in forest pools;
hunted among the laurel
and whispered to by swans
in accents of my own invention?

It is a dangerous time.
The water rocks away the timber
and here is your visa stamped in red.
You lean down your confident head.
We exchange kisses; I call your name
and wave you off as the bridge goes under.

Curiously, again allusions to Greek mythology, to Narcissus, Daphne, and Leda crop up, although here they are suggested by the actual I. A. Richards text referred to in the second stanza. Again, a prevailing formal pattern with more widely spaced rhymes. This time, the separation is viewed as a metaphorical journey. The daughter is not traveling off to boarding school, as one reviewer suggested. She is undertaking the rites of passage, making the necessary crossing from the innocence of childhood to the acute self-consciousness of adolescence. In her new life she will converse with her peers in their own patois. She goes forth armoured with the correct costume and the correct appurtenances. The sea, that sad, dying, all-mothering ocean that she must cross, is seen as "uncertain"; the time is "dangerous." But the daughter goes forth confidently, her visa (the menarche) already validated. No turning back. The bridge between mother and child serves no further function and it goes under.

There seems, perhaps a common enough phenomenon, to have been less fear on the poet's part that her daughters would be able to make the transition than fear for the fate of her son. In the following poem, rhythmically imitative of Auden, the poet remembers the boy's birth and the heroic measures required in the hospital to keep him breathing. No literary allusions here. The trimeter line and the *abab* rhyme scheme doubled or even trebled provide the reinforcing rods. The poet still likes this antique and sentimental poem. If only she could retract that dreadful "kiss" / "this" final couplet!

Poem for My Son

Where water laps my hips
it licks your chin. You stand
on tiptoe looking up
and swivel on my hands.
We play at this and laugh,
but understand you weigh
now almost less than life
and little more than sea.
So fine a line exists
between buoyance and stone
that, catching at my wrists,
I feel love notch the bone
to think you might have gone.

To think they smacked and pumped
to squall you into being
when you swam down, lungs limp
as a new balloon, and dying.
Six years today they bent
a black tube through your chest.

The tank hissed in the tent.
I leaned against the mast
outside that sterile nest.

And now inside the sea
you bump along my arm,
learning the narrow way
you've come from that red worm.
I tell you, save your air
and let the least swell ease you.
Put down, you flail for shore.
I cannot bribe nor teach you
to know the wet will keep you.

And cannot tell myself
unfasten from the boy.
On the Atlantic shelf
I see you wash away
to war or love or luck,
prodigious king, a stranger.
Times I stepped on a crack
my mother was in danger,
and time will find the chinks
to work the same in me.
You bobbled in my flanks.
They cut you from my sea.
Now you must mind your way.

Once, after a long swim
come overhand and wheezy
across the dappled seam
of lake, I foundered, dizzy,
uncertain which was better:
to fall there and unwind
in thirty feet of water
or fight back for the land.
Life would not let me lose it.
It yanked me by the nose.
Blackfaced and thick with vomit
it thrashed me to my knees.
We only think we choose.

But say we choose. Pretend it.
My pulse knit in your wrist
expands. Go now and spend it.
The sea will take our kiss.
Now, boy, swim off for this.

Here the poet seems to insist on, rather than protest over, her separation from the boy. She speculates today that the insistence was culturally imposed. Her expectations that the boy would "wash away / to war or love or luck, / prodigious king, a stranger" seem to her now to have been the standard maternal expectations of her era and should be viewed in that historical context. Nevertheless, it is painful to be old enough to speak of her past as an era.

In this poem the sea is a buoying but treacherous mother. Learning to float in it is a terrifying experience for the small boy who so nearly drowned at birth when fluid seeped into his lungs. Amnion and ocean both sustain and imperil. The poet remembers an incident when she too nearly drowned and discovered thereby how fierce the will to live, so fierce that she concludes we operate by instinct; "we only think we choose." She ends in a rhetorical burst, urging her small son forward metaphorically to make his own way on the strength of his genetic and God-knows-what-other inheritance. It is an overblown conclusion to an otherwise decent poem.

There is another motif. It emerges with the second book, *The Privilege*, published in 1965. For its epigraph the poet has taken some sentences from Joseph Conrad, who wrote to his aunt: "That's how it is! One must drag the ball and chain of one's selfhood to the end. It is the price one pays for the devilish and divine privilege of thought. . . ."

In two elegies for her father the poet comes again upon the desperate issue of autonomy, the ongoing and always paradoxical struggle for an identity separate from the parent. Now she looks back over her shoulder, as it were, at her own coming of age.

This is taken from "The Pawnbroker."

Firsthand I had from my father a love ingrown
tight as an oyster and returned it
as secretly. From him firsthand
the grace of work, the sweat of it, the bone-
tired unfolding down from stress.
I was the bearer he paid up on demand
with one small pearl of selfhood. Portionless,
I am oystering still to earn it.

Not of the House of Rothschild, my father, my creditor
lay dead while they shaved his cheeks and blacked his mustache.
My lifetime appraiser, my first prince whom death unhorsed
lay soberly dressed and barefoot to be burned.
That night, my brothers and I forced
the cap on his bottle of twenty-year-old scotch
and drank ourselves on fire beforehand
for the sacrament of closing down the hatch,
for the sacrament of casing down the ways
my thumb-licking peeler of cash on receipt of the merchandise,

possessor of miracles left unredeemed on the shelf
after thirty days,
giver and lender, no longer in hock to himself,
ruled off the balance sheet,
a man of great personal order
and small white feet.

Again, a strict rhyming pattern, a kind of enabling legislation to write the poem. It is interesting in retrospect to see the ocean once again, though obliquely, contained in the image of oyster and pearl and picked up on as a metaphor for the burial rites. In this instance, closing the lid on the father's body in the coffin is seen as the final act of battening down the hatches before setting sail. But the funeral is at the same time a beginning, a christening of a new ship for a new voyage as it is eased down the ways into the ocean.

Fortunately, the poet interjects, these illuminations of intent are not present at the time of composition.

A second elegy, "Lately, at Night," written in alternating twelve and fourteen-line stanzas in a looser rhyme scheme, deals more directly with the funeral parlor experience, the business of burial: "I am pulled up short / between those two big boys your sons, my brothers / brave as pirates putting into / a foreign port." Even in death, it seems, the father's domain can only be entered by an act of plunder. Autonomy is arrived at by piracy. And the final stanza, expressing the anguish of the separated child who is condemned to relive the dying man's last hours in her dreams, returns to the pirate ship metaphor:

> Father,
> lately at night as I watch your chest
> to help it to breathe in
> and swear it moves, and swear I hear the air
> rising and falling,
> even in the dream it is my own fat lungs
> feeding themselves, greedy as ever.
> Smother, drown or burn, Father,
> Father, no more false moves, I beg you.
> Back out of my nights, my dear dead undergroundling.
> It is time. Let the pirates berth their ships,
> broach casks, unload the hold, and let
> the dead skin of your forehead
> be a cold coin under my lips.

The poet would define these two themes—loss of the parent, relinquishment of the child—as central to her work. Once established they thrive like house plants but tend to branch off or hybridize as they grow.

By 1970, in *The Nightmare Factory*, the figure of the father is clearly an historical one, as in this excerpt from a poem called "The New York Times."

> Sundays my father
> hairs sprouting out of
> the V of his pajamas
> took in the sitdowns
> picket lines Pinkertons
> Bundists lend-lease
> under his mustache.
>
> In with the hash browns
> in with the double yolked
> once over lightly eggs
> mouthfuls of bad news.
> Nothing has changed, Poppa.
> The same green suburban lawn.
> The same fat life.

And the children are almost adults. The son, restless, disaffected, leaves home in a figurative sense. The mother is no longer an authority figure; she is helpless against the urgency of his craving to be gone:

> Today the jailbird maple in the yard
> sends down a thousand red hands in the rain.
> Trussed at the upstairs window I
> watch the great drenched leaves flap by
> knowing that on the comely boulevard
> incessant in your head you stand again
> at the cloverleaf, thumb crooked outward.
>
> Dreaming you travel light
> guitar pick and guitar

bedroll sausage-tight
they take you as you are.

They take you as you are
there's nothing left behind
guitar pick and guitar
on the highways of your mind.

Even the tree has been taken prisoner. The mother
too is captive, "trussed" at the window. She can only
speculate about her son's future:

How it will be tomorrow is anyone's guess.
The Rand McNally opens at a nudge
to forty-eight contiguous states, easy
as a compliant girl. In Minneapolis
I see you drinking wine under a bridge.
I see you turning on in Washington, D.C.,
panhandling in New Orleans, friendless

in Kansas City in an all-night beanery
and mugged on the beach in Venice outside L.A.
They take your watch and wallet and crack your head
as carelessly as an egg. The yolk runs red.
All this I see, or say it's what I see
in leaf fall, in rain, from the top of the stairs today
while your maps, those sweet pastels, lie flat and ready.
["For My Son on the Highways of His Mind"]

They are locked into this pattern, the mother and son,
he to take part in the "on the road" ethos of the sixties,
she to stand by grieving in the stereotype of mothers
everywhere. The refrain lines, two trimeter quatrains,
echo that early poem, "Poem for My Son." Indeed, the
poet had wished to write the entire poem in trimeter, but
found that the expository material was so dense that she
had to fall back from the lyric line into iambic penta-

meter, which is far better adapted to the kinds of cataloging she felt she needed to do.

In a sense, while the mother-son relationship has simplified itself, the mother-daughter one has grown more complicated. A darker outline emerges. It is no longer a matter of waving the child off into adolescence. Now the poet must deal with a necessary rivalry developing between mother and daughter, which ends, as it must, with the metaphorical dismissal and death of the mother.

Metaphor is not smaller than life. It mediates between awesome truths. It leaps up from instinctual feeling bearing forth the workable image. Thus in a sense the metaphor is truer than the actual fact.

In "Father's Song" the poet draws distinctions between the father's attitude toward the son and toward the daughters. It is a feudal poem, not one the poet would wish to save, but it points a direction:

> I have not said there is the season
> of tantrums when the throats of doors are cut
> with cold slammings. Rooms fill with tears.
> The bedclothes drown in blood
> for these will be women. They will lie down
> with lovers, they will cry out giving birth,
> they will grow old with hard knuckles and dry necks.
> Death will punish them with subtractions.
> They will burn me and put me into the earth.

Although the persona is that of the male parent, the feeling tone clearly is shared with the mother.

Again, in "The Fairest One of All," which alludes to, indeed depends for its effect on the grisly outcome of this fairy tale, the premonition of her own death calls forth from the poet this concluding stanza to a love poem for her older daughter:

So far so good, my darling, my fair
first born, your hair black as ebony
your lips red as blood. But let there be
no mistaking how the dark scheme runs.
Too soon all this will befall:
Too soon the huntsman will come.
He will bring me the heart of a wild boar
and I in error will have it salted and cooked
and I in malice will eat it bit by bit
thinking it yours.
And as we both know, at the appropriate moment
I will be consumed by an inexorable fire
as you look on.

The poet is given courage to press on by Yeats, who
wrote: "I must lie down where all the ladders start / In
the foul rag and bone shop of the heart." For these are
harsh judgments, that the daughters, to come of age,
must psychologically overwhelm their mothers, that they
must cannibalize across the generations one on another.

With the publication of *House, Bridge, Fountain, Gate*
in 1975 the poet has, she now thinks, completed the
tasks. She has let go of the large children although she
returns thematically to them, evoking memory. In "The
Knot" she writes, addressing an absent daughter:

It's last summer in this picture, a day on the edge
of our time zone. We are standing in the park,
our genes declare themselves, death smiles in the sun
streaking the treetops, the sky all lightstruck . . .
In the dark you were packed about with toys,
you were sleeping on your knees, never alone
your breathing making little o's
of trust, night smooth as soapstone
and the hump of your bottom like risen bread . . .

and ends, coming to terms with the separation in time as
well as place:

> . . . I chew on the knot
> we were once. Meanwhile, your eyes, serene
> in the photo, look most thoughtfully out
> and could be bullet holes, or beauty spots.

Similarly, in a poem addressed to the foster son who still searches for his lost mother, she admonishes:

> It is true that we lie down on cowflops
> praying they'll turn into pillows.
> It is true that our mothers explode
> out of the snowballs of dreams
> or speak to us down the chimney
> saying our names above the wind
>
> or scrape their legs like crickets
> in the dead grass behind the toolshed
> tapping a code we can't read.
>
> That a man may be free of his ghosts
> he must return to them like a garden.
> He must put his hands in the sweet rot
> uprooting the turnips, washing them
> tying them into bundles
> and shouldering the whole load to market.
>   ["History Lesson"]

Perhaps what she has said of the young man's ghosts can also be said of her own? Hasn't this been the informing thrust of her poetry? Particularly in this book she "returns to them like a garden"; she has spread out the decade of the thirties in which she was a small child, all of its "sweet rot" exposed. Nor does it matter which details are invented, which are recorded. If everything coheres, the poem has been served. Here is the central stanza from "The Thirties Revisited," full of those warring misconceptions:

Now I am ten. Enter Mamselle,
my mother's cut-rate milliner.
She is putting her eyes out in the hall
at thirty cents an hour
tacking veils onto felt forms.
Mamselle is an artist.
She can copy the Eiffel Tower
in feathers with a rolled-up brim.
She can make pyramids out of cherries.
Mamselle wears cheese boxes on her feet.
Madame can buy and sell her.

If daughters were traded among the accessories
in the perfumed hush of Bonwit Teller's
she'd have replaced me with a pocketbook,
snapped me shut and looped me over
her Hudson seal cuff: me of the chrome-wire mouth,
the inkpot braids, one eye that looks
wrongly across at the other.
O Lady of the Chaise Longue,
O Queen of the Kimono,
I disappoint my mother.

Yet it is in this collection that the poet begins—she is a
late beginner!—to come to terms with the ways in which
her own mother was shaped by the social constraints of
her young womanhood. "Life's Work," "Sperm," "The
Deaths of the Uncles," narrative poems of some length,
take up the tantalizing mythology of her mother's family:

O Grandfather, look what your seed has done!
Look what has come of those winter night gallops.
You tucking the little wife up
under the comforter that always leaked feathers.
You coming perhaps just as the trolley
derailed taking the corner at 15th Street
in a shower of sparks, and Grandmother's
corset spread out like a filleted fish
to air meanwhile on the window sill.

She will make Galsworthian figures of them all, willy-nilly. In "Life's Work" she contrasts her mother's rebellion against the aforementioned stern grandfather with her own efforts to break away. Her mother, denied a musical career, eloped with the man who became the poet's father. Characteristically, when faced with his daughter's ambitions, he

> swore on the carrots and the boiled beef
> that I would come to nothing
> that I would come to grief . . .
>
> the midnights of my childhood still go on
> the stairs speak again under your foot
> the heavy parlor door folds shut
> and "Au Clair de la Lune"
> puckers from the obedient keys
> plain as a schoolroom clock ticking
> and what I hear more clearly than Debussy's
> lovesong is the dry aftersound
> of your long nails clicking.

So the mother is not the villain after all? So we are victims of our dailiness, in whatever archetypal roles we are cast? As Jung tells us, there will always be the mother, the father, the miraculous child. Everything we construct arises from these primordial images, very possibly inborn in us. The poet is still doing her homework in the human psyche. The children continue to appear in virtually every new work she undertakes, sometimes viewed with acceptance, sometimes with distance. In "Changing the Children" she concludes:

> Eventually we get them back.
> Now they are grown up.
> They are much like ourselves.
> They wake mornings beyond cure,

not a virgin among them.
We are civil to one another.
We stand in the kitchen
slicing bread, drying spoons
and tuning in to the weather.

"Sunbathing on a Rooftop in Berkeley" is addressed, some fifteen years later, to the same daughter as was "The Journey." But the lines are open and adopt a more relaxed, conversational tone. Stanzas match but there is no rhyme scheme. The poet thinks her tone is no more or less assured working in this freer way. She thinks only that it befits the material, that the collision of particulars, observed and recalled, build up to and prepare for the unvarnished truth of the ending:

O summers without end, the exact truth is
we are expanding sideways as haplessly
as in the mirrors of the Fun House.
We bulge toward the separate fates that await us,
sometimes touching, as sleeves will, whether
or not a hug was intended.

O summers without end, the truth is
no matter how I love her, Death
blew up my dress that day
while she was in the egg unconsidered.

The poet wishes to make one final entry in this often awkward disquisition on herself. A recent poem, "The Envelope," grew out of a chance encounter with a phrase from Heidegger, "the fear of cessation." It was that curious Latinate usage, although very likely the Latinism was acquired in translation, that triggered the opening line and a half. The rest of the poem was carried forth by the poet's ongoing preoccupation with the tribal notion of succession. Her preoccupation, she concedes, is ever more heavily tinged with intimations of her own mortality. Nevertheless, the poet here records her perpetual astonishment at her good fortune in having had daughters. In addition to the esthetic and emotional pleasure they provide, she feels agreeably improved on by them.

The Envelope

It is true, Martin Heidegger, as you have written,
I fear to cease, even knowing that at the hour
of my death my daughters will absorb me, even
knowing they will carry me about forever
inside them, an arrested fetus, even as I carry
the ghost of my mother under my navel, a nervy
little androgynous person, a miracle
folded in lotus position.

Like those old pear-shaped Russian dolls that open
at the middle to reveal another and another, down
to the pea-sized, irreducible minim,
may we carry our mothers forth in our bellies.
May we, borne onward by our daughters, ride
in the Envelope of Almost-Infinity,
that chain letter good for the next twenty-five
thousand days of their lives.

The womanly images persist. Just as there is an ovum in "Sunbathing..." there is the fetus within the womb here. But a peculiar transformation has taken place in the childbearing process. Now it is our mothers, as well as our children, whom we carry about with us, internalized *lares* and *penates*, as it were. The poem concludes as a prayer of sorts. Clearly, the poet's ego is speaking. She wants to outlast her time frame. She prays to be carried on.

III
Three Lectures on Poetry

These three pieces were prepared for oral presentation to a large general audience at the Bread Loaf Writers' Conference. They span the years 1969 to 1977. If their tone is uncomfortably hortatory on the page, the intent was to rouse novitiates in poetry to their best efforts.

Closing the Door

My subject today is the matter of ending a poem. I confess that I am growing rather curmudgeonly on the issue of endings, wanting as I do some definitive and actual sense of closure. If not the slam of the door at the end of the poem, which Oscar Williams speaks of, then at least the click of the bolt in the jamb. My bête noire is the poem that ends by simply falling off the page in an accident of imbalance, so that the reader, poor fish, doesn't actually know the poem has ended. He turns the page in expectation of further enlightenment, only to be caught red-fingered with the title of the next poem coldly sizing him up.

Nor does it matter, I think, whether we are talking about the vatic, oracular poet whose poems come in a kind of seizure as Blake's did, or as Richard Eberhart's do, or whether we are talking about the carefully crafted poems which A. E. Housman carried around for weeks in his head before writing them down, something Richard Wilbur also does (as he says, "in a state of warm self-indulgence"), or as I imagine John Crowe Ransom did. A poem may be written at one sitting or it may lie around in a pile of thoughts for months or years before coming to being. The finished poem, whatever its wellspring, has been raised to its highest intensity, has passed the fulcrum, the hinge part if you will, and now comes to its conclusion. It has always seemed to me that some lapses can be forgiven the poet if he finishes well, just as they can be forgiven the lover. I will of course be accused by some of having fallen victim to a bad case of formalism, as if to end well or to end declaratively were a disease of technical cunning. I can only plead, if this be technical cunning, make the most of it.

One way of ending the poem is to turn it back on itself, like a serpent with its tail in its mouth. Robert Frost comes immediately to mind. Many of his poems are circular, wind back on themselves, sometimes growing out of the demands of form, as in "Stopping by Woods on a Snowy Evening," where the repeated line is an inspired act of desperation, the only way to break out of the established dilemma. You will remember how each stanza introduces a new rhyme word which is then carried along into the next stanza. The rhyming pattern appears deceptively simple, but by the antepenultimate stanza, it becomes evident that the poet is trapped in his built-in infinity factor. His solution—to tie the poem together with the repeat of "And miles to go before I sleep"—not only invests the line with another and darker layer of meaning, but satisfies the ear, completes the statement, and closes the door.

Other circular Frost poems suggest themselves: "The Road Not Taken," "I Have Been One Acquainted with the Night," and one which has long been a favorite with me, "Provide, Provide." In this case the title is wrapped around to become the final line of the poem. The self-contained, enveloping force of the poem is greatly intensified by the fact that the poem is written in triplets, generally considered a rhyme scheme more suited to light verse than to a voice as fiercely elegiac as this one: "Better to go down dignified / With boughten friendship at your side / Than none at all. Provide, provide."

I don't mean to suggest by these examples that form alone can dictate an ending—this is far from the case. But I am formalist enough in my own work and inclination to find myself turning almost by default to poems that rise and fall on the iron struts of their structures. The advantage of working in form as a discipline is that it throws the poet back on the language. Roethke has said that it forces him to be aware of the fluidity of words, of how he can shape the sentence to a particular end. This can go either way. He can embrace the form or resist it— "either result can be useful." And Wilbur, preferring to work in form, has explained that without the preexistence of a norm one cannot recognize subtle variations. Form requires the poet to take greater pains in the choice and disposition of words, because it slows down and makes more complicated the writing process. Such limitation, Wilbur feels, makes for power: "the strength of the genie comes of his being confined in a bottle."

Some poems can depend on sound and repetition, rather than on rhyme, for their end effect. In this connection I think of one familiar to many of you, as it is much anthologized, Henry Reed's "Naming of Parts." I won't quote it all, but remind you of the subject, the raw recruit receiving introduction in the manual of arms. The poem turns on a lovely artless play between the parade of spring burgeoning with all its sexual overtones and the mechanical lesson in how to kill that is being presented. It begins:

> Today we have naming of parts. Yesterday,
> We had daily cleaning. And tomorrow morning,

We shall have what to do after firing. But today,
Today we have naming of parts. Japonica
Glistens like coral in all of the neighbouring gardens,
And today we have naming of parts.

Reed proceeds through the lower sling swivel, the safety catch, the bolt, and the breech, and concludes:

They call it easing the Spring: it is perfectly easy
If you have any strength in your thumb: like the bolt,
And the breech, and the cocking-piece, and the point of
    balance,
Which in our case we have not got; and the almond-blossom
Silent in all of the gardens and the bees going backwards and
    forwards,
For today we have naming of parts.

Or, for another example, the poem, "Visit to St. Elizabeth's," by Elizabeth Bishop, a poem which protests the incarceration of Ezra Pound in this mental institution in Washington, D.C. The format of the poem echoes, one might say mocks, the nursery rhyme, "this is the house that Jack built." It builds from the one-line opening stanza, "This is the house of Bedlam," through the second stanza, like an add-a-pearl necklace, "This is the man / that lies in the house of Bedlam," down to the final stanza, which begins:

This is a soldier home from the war.
These are the years and the walls and the door
that shut on a boy that pats the floor

and continues through a series of linkages to build the crazy-house scene.

Not only does this poem depend structurally on the device of repetition, but it also leans very heavily, I think, on the word "that" used as a depersonalized substitute for the pronoun "who." Cumulative repetition rises here to a controlled scream, as it were, at the end.

A small lyrical statement, remarkable, I think for the precision of the imagery, is "The Even Sea," by May Swenson.

The Even Sea

Meekly the sea
now plods to shore:
white-faced cattle used to their yard,
the waves, with weary knees,
come back from bouldered hills
of high water,

where all the gray, rough day they seethed like bulls,
till the wind laid down its goads
at shift of tide, and sundown
gentled them; with lowered necks
they amble up the beach
as to their stalls.

There is not a great thrust here, but a quiet shaping of the expectation stated in the opening line: "Meekly the sea now plods to shore." The poet moves the poem backward in time to the day now past, and comes forward at the end to close where she began—the waves like cattle "amble up the beach / as to their stalls." It is an exercise in what I like to call poetic tact: a small subject, and a low-keyed one, treated in firm, unsentimental terms and not forced beyond its natural boundaries. Here, the metaphor controls the closure. The end is determined by the internal logic of the prevailing image.

Next, to set up another artifical category, let us consider poems which end with the understatement that startles or arouses. A sterling example is the magnificently cadent poem by Auden, "Musée des Beaux Arts," which soars, incident by incident, from the general opening statement, "About suffering they were never wrong, / The Old Masters," to the final stately measured beat, "and the expensive delicate ship that must have seen / Something amazing, a boy falling out of the sky, / Had somewhere to get to and sailed calmly on."

The poem moves in a kind of spiral from its general and abstract opening statement about the famous painters whose works hang in this museum to the specifics contained within the paintings. The workings of chance or fate are visited on a cross section of individuals, including, perforce, tragic accidents, drownings, deaths, even "the dreadful martyrdom," never more closely defined than that. It doesn't have to be, because of the clinching details that follow it—the dogs that "go on with their doggy life and the torturer's horse [that] scratches its innocent behind on a tree." Through the alchemy of the poetic and painterly arts, these events coexist: the torturer works his cruelty at the same moment that the passive horse grazes all unaware, scratching his itches.

The purity of the description prepares, I think, for the succeeding stanza in which Auden reproduces exactly the Breughel scene. The drowning of Icarus is not an important failure, any more than is the drowning of the children or the anguish of the tortured victim. So, overtly, says the poem. But of course the poet is saying exactly the opposite. He is saying that they all matter, that each man's death or suffering is equally significant. The death of the child is as important as the death of Icarus, even though the drowning is simply a random, meaningless event in the frame of things, and the drowning of Icarus symbolizes a deliberate fateful punishment for a transgression. Icarus committed the sin of hubris, of overweening pride, by daring the gods on his wax wings; his falling into the sea serves as a warning and an example.

The plain, flatly spoken ending, in all its cagey simplicity, is very Audenesque. The word choice of "expensive, delicate ship," so toylike, so elegant, so miniaturized, is apt indeed. So is the simple language of "must have seen something amazing, a boy falling out of the sky"—not the cometlike descent of a gleaming, heroic figure swathed in wax feathers, none of that—just the dry, understated shock of exactly what was seen, and all the human disregard of the plight of others that is contained in it. The ship had somewhere to get to and sailed on.

The point of understatement is that it can so often create an effect that hyperbole would destroy. It makes me think of Auden's reply to Walter Kerr who had asked him, during an interview, to discuss the relationship of artifice to sincerity in life. Auden answered by comparing sincerity to falling asleep. "I mean if you try too hard, you won't." Perhaps this is applicable to the problem of ending a poem. Often the quiet and deliberately flat sentence does the work of a dozen implied exclamation points.

Sometimes when understatement comes well laced with irony, the effect can be quite savage, as in a poem titled "Does It Matter?" by a British poet of the First World War, Siegfried Sassoon. Each of the three stanzas opens with the question the title poses. In the first instance Sassoon asks, "Does it matter?—losing your legs? . . . / For people will always be kind." The second stanza repeats the pattern, except that the soldier has been blinded in battle. The final stanza alludes to a soldier suffering from shell shock, "those dreams from the pit." In each case the soldier is assured that "people will always be kind" even as the poet contrasts the legless veteran with his robust friends who return from fox-hunting, or recommends splendid projects to the blind man. The victim of shell shock is blithely assured that his most disturbed acts will be forgiven on grounds that he has fought for his country; therefore, "no one will worry a bit."

Or this even more elementary example of the uses to which understatement can be put in closure from our lowercase poet, e. e. cummings, who specialized in pricking the balloons of bombast as he deranged typography and line breaks and utterly demolished punctuation. In "next to of course god america i" he has constructed an entire poem of phrases drawn from a typical Fourth of July oration. Snatches from our national anthem and lyrics from other American patriotic songs commingle as the poem rushes headlong into the rhetorical question asked in its penultimate line, "then shall the voice of liberty be mute?" The last line closes the poem and turns the text on its ear: "He spoke. And drank rapidly a glass of water."

It is worth pointing out that cummings's poem is a sonnet, tightly rhymed, that all except the final line is enclosed in quotation marks to indicate the voice of the speaker, and that the last line is set apart by normal punctuation and capitalization so as to underscore the irony of the situation.

One further example of understatement is to be found in Randall Jarrell's well-known, much-anthologized little poem, "The Death of the Ball Turret Gunner," which first appeared in a collection published in 1945. It is appropriate today, I think, to explain that a ball turret was a plexiglass bubble that was set in the belly of a B-17 or B-24 Flying Fortress or Liberator Bomber. Only a short man could curl himself, fetal position, into this sphere; he was particularly vulnerable to attck. When struck, his body was reduced to spaghetti.

Now let us consider Jarrell's last line and see how forcefully, yet with deliberate understatement, with deliberate refusal to hoke up the level of language it works: "When I died they washed me out of the turret with a hose." It is awesome in its simplicity. It produces an effect that hyperbole would destroy. All the despair of mankind at the destructive power unleashed in war is contained in it.

Another kind of ending suggests itself to me—the poem that makes a prophetic or apocalyptic statement at the end, as for example Yeats's final summation in his famous poem, "The Second Coming," which begins: "Turning and turning in the widening gyre," and ends, "What great beast, his hour come round at last, / Slouches toward Bethlehem to be born?" Or the equally well-known Matthew Arnold poem, "Dover Beach," with its rich tone of desolation: "The sea is calm tonight / The tide is full, the moon lies fair / Upon the straits" that builds to the thundering drama of the conclusion:

> Ah, love, let us be true
> To one another! for the world, which seems
> To lie before us like a land of dreams,
> So various, so beautiful, so new
> Hath really neither joy, nor love, nor light,
> Nor certitude, nor peace, nor help for pain;
> And we are here as on a darkling plain
> Swept with confused alarms of struggle and flight,
> Where ignorant armies clash by night.

However awesome, I feel this kind of ending—a grand clash of cymbals—is the most difficult to bring off. It calls forth an explosion of feeling, a wave of collective excitement that is swept along to a powerful declarative finale, something like the finale of a Beethoven symphony. Perhaps this kind of closure belongs more surely to the masters—who but an Eliot could have written: "This is the way the world ends, / this is the way the world ends, / this is the way the world ends, / not with a bang but a whimper"? For despite the whimper word, it is a ringing, declarative final statement. Or Milton, concluding his "When I Consider How My Life Is Spent" with the resonant words spoken by Patience personified: "They also serve who only stand and wait."

For a more contemporary example, take Robert Lowell's poem about Jonathan Edwards, "Mr. Edwards and the Spider," in which the fierce moralist and theologian, observing the insect, muses on life's end. I'll quote just the last of it, a hellfire sermon directed against a particular sinner.

> Josiah Hawley, picture yourself cast
> Into a brick-kiln where the blast
> Fans your quick vitals to a coal—
> If measured by a glass,
> How long would it seem burning! Let there pass
> A minute, ten, ten trillion; but the blaze
> Is infinite, eternal: this is death,
> To die and know it. This is the Black Widow, death.

I don't mean to group only the dark endings together as poems which turn on a sense of prophecy or plea or intimation of the apocalypse. There is Marvell's "To His Coy Mistress," ending on the beautiful defiance of: "Thus though we cannot make our sun / Stand still, yet we will make him run." Richard Wilbur's poem, "Love Calls Us to the Things of This World," functions, I think, in much the same way, although it closes on a hallelujah rather than a groan. In it the poet observes the washing dancing out the slum windows of Rome on a series of pulley lines. After an almost tranced series of descriptions in which the laundry comes to life, he concludes, acknowledging all human needs and strivings:

The soul descends once more in bitter love
To accept the waking body, saying now
In a changed voice as the man yawns and rises,

"Bring them down from their ruddy gallows;
Let there be clean linen for the backs of thieves;
Let lovers go fresh and sweet to be undone,
And the heaviest nuns walk in a pure floating
Of dark habits,
           keeping their difficult balance."

And finally, the category I think of as poems which end on an aggressive shift of balance at the end, closing the door with an unexpected shiver, the shiver of recognition we undergo when the line or lines are apt, however surprising. Most of Edward Arlington Robinson's poems would fall neatly into this pigeonhole. Remember, for instance, the ending of "Richard Cory":

So on we worked, and waited for the light
And went without the meat and cursed the bread
And Richard Cory, one calm summer night
Went home and put a bullet through his head.

But there are poems which shift or startle without relying on so heavy an ironic twist. For example, consider the preparation for the surprise of the ending in the Sexton poem, "For My Lover Returning to His Wife." It contains these lines:

Let's face it. I have been momentary.
A luxury. A bright red sloop in the harbor.
My hair rising like smoke from the car window.
Littleneck clams out of season

as contrasted with the portrait of the wife:

she is your have to have . . .
She is so naked and singular.
She is the sum of yourself and your dream.
Climb her like a monument, step after step.
She is solid.

As for me, I am a watercolor.
I wash off.

And here, to take another contemporary but less
known example, a poem called "Award" by Ray Durem.
It has as its epigraph this message: "A gold watch to the
FBI Man who has followed me for 25 years."

Well, old spy
looks like I
led you down some pretty blind alleys,
took you on several trips to Mexico,
fishing in the high Sierras,
jazz at the Philharmonic.
You've watched me all your life,
I've clothed your wife,
put your two sons through college.
What good has it done?
The sun keeps rising every morning.
Ever see me buy an assistant President?
or close a school?
or lend money to Trujillo?

ever catch me rigging airplane prices?
I bought some after-hours whiskey in L.A.
but the Chief got his pay.
I ain't killed no Koreans
or fourteen-year-old boys in Mississippi.
neither did I bomb Guatemala,
or lend guns to shoot Algerians.
I admit I took a Negro child
to a white rest room in Texas,
but she was my daughter, only three,
who had to pee.

Such an ending has the virtue of catching us not quite unaware, for the polemical tone has prepared us to some extent, but we are caught by the flat, palms-up declaration. The antilyrical thrust is what I would call it, and it is a style considerably sought after these days.

Let us conclude, then, back where we began. All poems must close, even those that posit an infinity as the Frost poems do. Many poems succeed in shutting the door by turning back on themselves to unite beginning and ending. Pattern, rhyme, form of some sort probably serve their strongest purpose in this behest. It is possible for the poet to come down on an understatement that jars us to some apprehension of the truth; it is possible but perhaps more difficult to achieve the same goal with the anchor of prophecy, prayer, or shadow of the apocalypse. It is perhaps even harder to attain by turning or shifting the focus or tone or intent of the poem with a socket wrench just at the end.

Coming Across

Establishing the Intent of a Poem

How do poems begin? Who really knows? "How do I love you, let me count the ways" is probably as good an answer as any. The impulse to build a poem may be something amorphous, inchoate, vague yet persistent as a floating sense of unease. It may be an emotion as specific as anger, as explicit as the sex drive, as necessary as food. The poet may start with a fact or feeling. He may be the kind of writer who knows from the outset what he is aiming at, or he may be the kind who at the moment of particularly heightened tension in a peculiar aura seizes his chaos or prickly perception and seeks to interpret it, make some sort of order out of it, never knowing really where the muse will lead him.

I think most poets have had both kinds of experience—the immediate palpable need to get a poem down whole, and the other, formless but equally valid urge to follow wherever the words and feelings lead. Once in a great while the "given" poem comes along, the *don*, the gift, a poem that flows easily. It proceeds onto the page as if it had been shaped by the seraphim up there on the golden pavement and lightly handed down to the poet simply to record. It is like admitting to having had an earthly visitation to get such a poem—three times in ten years this has happened to me—and each time I was totally unprepared for the event. Much more often there is the sweat and wrestle of tearing the poem out of experience and struggling to get it into being. Barry Spacks has immortalized this process in a little poem.

The Muse

The Muse came pulling off her gown
And nine feet tall she laid her down
And I by her side a popinjay
With nothing to say.
Did she mean to stay?

She smelled like flame, like starch on sweat,
Like sperm, like shame, like a launderette.
No one, she said, has loved me right.
Day and night. Day and night.

Spacks here is describing ironically and in a delightful self-mocking tone the visitation that doesn't quite come off. The muse comes, all right, and she is an Amazon of a lady before whom the poet quails, filled with feelings of unworthiness or inadequacy. Is he up to the necessary courtship? Will she stay? She is redolent of elemental drives: she smells "like flame, like starch on sweat, / like sperm, like shame, like a launderette"—and he is the poor fish who is expected to give voice, give life to these basic and vital items. Then, when the lady speaks, the mask falls away and she does so in the querulous tone of an unsatisfied woman. No one, she says, has loved me right. Day and night, day and night. The muse's statement, indeed the whole poem, becomes then a metaphor for the inability of the poet ever quite to fulfill his inspiration. No one ever realizes his highest potential. Man, that pseudoperfectible being, never quite attains his godhood.

How can we ever live up to our muse, that demanding, petulant Junoesque creature who comes, pulling off her gown? The honest and obvious answer is simply that we can't, or at least that we rarely can. The dissatisfied poet ought to take some comfort, though, from the very fact of his dissatisfaction. The worst sin is complacency. We can't afford to be smug about what we write. We need always to ask ourselves of a poem, yes, but does it work? Does it do what we wanted it to do, excite sympathy, anger, lift the reader out of his chair? Does it *come across*? What is the intent of the poem and how is it established?

Let's look at a poem by Randall Jarrell, titled "Eighth Air Force." The poem is very open-faced. It describes in detail a group of World War II soldiers at rest between flying their bombing missions. There is the eternal puppy, that in other instances is a kitten, or sometimes a war waif, who has been adopted as company mascot. There are the flowers, a domestic touch, a hankering after beauty. There is the idle game being played, the ablution—shaving—being performed. There is the forgetfulness of booze, there is the terrible memory of missions past and the dread of missions to come, all of them adding up to the present one, one, one. All this is told through the voice of the speaker, one of the company, and it is told flatly, directly, resolutely. But what is Jarrell's intent? Is it simply to describe men at their leisure between air strikes, men who "play, before they die, / Like puppies with their puppy"?

It seems to me that the poem's intent becomes clear the minute we fall onto the allusion, *ecce homo*—behold the man. *Ecce homo* evokes Pontius Pilate pointing in all those paintings, Pontius Pilate who pleaded for Jesus's life, but not forcefully enough. We are induced by these details to remember the dream out of the Apocrypha, although it was Pontius's wife who dreamed it and then she harassed him further, poor man. It was Peter who lied three times before the cock crowed, but everything now coalesces in the poem to raise goosebumps on the arms of the reader. "Men wash their hands in blood, as best they can./I find no fault in this just man." It is all déjà vu—we have been here before, surely, at this washing of the hands. Now even the game of pitching pennies takes on a more sinister meaning, suggesting the Roman soldiers gambling under the cross. Here we all are playing this game of war, but like Pilate too weak to dissent from the general will or habit. Jarrell expresses an intense revulsion against war as a form of legal murder, of which he, the speaker, is as guilty as the rest of the soldiers. The poem is prophetic with Jarrell now dead; it speaks to the Vietnam war as vividly as any contemporary poem might. It is a poem that means to persuade and polemicize. It doesn't specifically say, "War is evil" or "War is hell" or "Just men will refuse to go forth and kill any longer" but that is the message the reader receives.

The effect is doubly powerful because it is implied rather than so stated. The poet shows, rather than tells. The shock of revulsion is intensified because the poet moves away from the direct recording of experience, poignant though that is, into an honorable literary (or more accurately, biblical) allusion and that allusion swoops down on us, bearing the full freight of our spiritual history. Notice I am speaking only of intent and tone, not of meter, rhyme, and language, though these are all germane to the topic and add to the coming across.

Lastly, a poem in the simplest possible, quiet, understated diction of Linda Pastan. It is called "Consolations."

Consolations

Listen:
language does the best it can.
I speak

the dog whines
and in the changeling trees
late bees mumble, vague

as voices
barely heard
from the next room.

Later
the consolations
of silence.

The nights pass slowly.
I turn their heavy pages
one by one

licking my index finger
as my grandfather did
wanting to close the book on pain.

Afternoons smell of burning.
Already leaves have loosened
on the branch

small scrolls bearing
the old messages
each year.

You touch me—
another language. Our griefs
are almost one;

we swing them between us
like the child lent us awhile
who holds one hand of yours

and one of mine
hurrying us home
as street lights

start to flower
down the dark stem
of evening.

This poem is written in free verse; it has no regular meter, although there is a stanzaic pattern. Most of the sentences are simple declarative statements—"I speak," "the dog whines," "Afternoons smell of burning," and so on. A contrast is being drawn between the sounds of language, language even with all its limitations, and what the poet calls "the consolations of silence." In silence, communications are conveyed in other, visual, tactile, olfactory ways, but conveyed nonetheless. She lists these, very quietly and quite obliquely, but with telling effect.

The intent of the poem and its emotive power depend heavily on what I will call the elegiac underlay. This poem, in common with virtually every lasting love lyric down the ages, casts before it the premonitory shadow of our mortality. The poignancy of the setting with its autumnal trees, of the participants, that man and woman and "the child lent us awhile" is contained wholly in the small capsule that is a lifetime. It is the presence of death that makes the moment meaningful, the knowledge of finite time that sharpens the edge of each image.

The intent, then, as I read it, parallels Matthew Arnold's anguished cry for solidarity between the lovers in "Dover Beach": "let us be true / To one another!" for ". . . we are here as on a darkling plain." But when Pastan says "Our griefs / are almost one" and goes on to turn that handsome simile of the child on loan, we are both caught up in the aptness of the image and arrested by the chilling, qualifying word *almost*. She has taken a frank and unsentimental look at the human condition. She is telling us that we are locked up in our individual autonomy, that we cannot, despite all manner of close bonds, go undifferentiated. Although touch functions as "another language," although the child between them "holds one hand of yours / and one of mine" the *I* of the poem acknowledges that neither language nor the consolations of silence can bridge entirely the gap that separates the lovers. They and their child must move inexorably "down the dark stem / of evening"; the coming on of darkness seems quite plainly here to serve as an archetypal image for the final closure of death.

Intent, as I read it, is something larger than the simple event or plot of the poem. I have a lot of narrow prejudices in this connection. I'm not very often satisfied with a straight imagist poem. For me a poem must go beyond its setting or its particular to say outright or by subtle suggestion something about man's universal condition. If the gift without the giver is bare, the poem without the concept is emaciated, merely a skeleton. I want, I am hungry for something elusive I can only call *realization*. I don't know another word for it except maybe to say that what I want of a poem is that it arouse in me a sympathetic response to its authenticity.

Four Kinds of *I*

Ben Shahn, in an essay I very much admire—the book is *The Shape of Content*, the essay, "The Biography of a Painting"—talks about a picture he exhibited in the late forties which he chose to call *Allegory*. A huge beast resembling the Greek Chimera haloed in flames arches across the figures of four children who are sprawled on the ground. That is the outer configuration of the painting. A critic whom Shahn admired and who until then had always dealt with him mercifully grew quite exercised about this painting. He attributed political motives to it, seeing it as some sort of symbol of Red Moscow, and ended, as Shahn reports it, by recommending that the artist, along with the Red Dean of Canterbury, be deported.

Well, it is my contention that the first personal singular, the voice of the *I* or *moi*, is often susceptible of the same kind of interpretation. And from time to time we have the parallel phenomenon of the critics calling for the equivalent of deportation for the guilty poet. Usually the attack centers on what has come loosely to be called confessional poetry, which for the sake of establishing a category I will more broadly name autobiographical poetry, whether or not the tone or substance lends itself to confession. But more of that later.

For the purposes of discussion, and without any wish to be held to the limits of these categories, I've chosen to divide the *I* poems into the lyric *I*, the persona *I*, the ideational *I*, and the autobiographical *I*. The lyric poems of the Greeks date among our very earliest literary artifacts. Lyrics were originally composed to be sung, or at least appropriate for singing; in all its various forms developed over centuries under diverse cultural influences, the lyric has always had as its basic identity a communicated personal feeling. Maybe the first lyric was a lament for a lost love or a paean of praise for a good harvest. But in any case, the communication of personal emotion remains central to the lyric, and the poet's job continues to be to undertake and make valid that communication. Often the feeling will be expressed obliquely or will be an amalgam of complex and even contradictory feelings that may require unusual treatment.

Thus a Dylan Thomas poem, "If I Were Tickled by the Rub of Love," passionately fuses the bardic romantic into a poem in praise of man, in praise of his mortality, his sensuality and his humanity. In 1950, three years before his untimely death, Thomas, parodying T. S. Eliot, summed up the essential qualities of his life saying: "First, I am a Welshman. Second, I am a drunkard. Third, I am heterosexual." The poem we now know by its opening line, "If I Were Tickled by the Rub of Love," plays almost prophetically on the theme of the poet's brief life offered in willing exchange for the pleasures of the flesh. Consider such hedonic images as the red tickle, the hatching hair, the winging bone, the urchin hungers, the lovers' rub, which—for he is not deceived— "wipes away not crow's-foot nor the lock / Of sick old manhood on the fallen jaws." And further, as he says, "I sit and watch the worm beneath my nail / Wearing the quick away." Here is the concluding stanza:

And what's the rub? Death's feather on the nerve?
Your mouth, my love, the thistle in the kiss?
My Jack of Christ born thorny on the tree?
The words of death are dryer than his stiff,
My wordy wounds are printed with your hair.
I would be tickled by the rub that is:
Man be my metaphor.

If we ask ourselves, what is the value of using the first-person voice in a lyric poem, we may come up with some interesting answers. Does the first-person voice give a greater illusion of reality, does it intensify the power of the emotion being expressed? How would it work if Thomas had written: If *man* were tickled by the rub of love, or if *one* were so tickled? When a first-person narrator is in charge, the selection of details is in a sense simplified, much as it is in the general convention of fiction. The narrator reports only what he knows about. His perceptions are limited, narrowed, but undoubtedly enhanced by his first-hand account of them.

Of course, when a first-person narrator tells about things which he himself doesn't really understand but the audience does, he employs an effective ironic device. The purpose of the irony is to stress the gap between appearance and reality. For instance, a poem by John Crowe Ransom called "Piazza Piece" is written in two voices, the voice of a young girl, the "lady young in beauty waiting," and in the voice of an old man, "a gentleman in a dustcoat trying / To make you hear." It's a persona, or masque, poem, in which the poet assumes the voice of another. In this case, two voices play against each other in the octet and sestet of a sonnet.

It is an Italian or Petrarchan sonnet, obedient to the limited rhyme scheme of that form. Historically, the Italian sonnet, which Petrarch used to communicate his love for Laura, took the form of pseudolamentation—the beloved is fair but unattainable, she scorns the poet's amorous advances—and it was all a game, an amusing, entertaining play of words, which Reason turns inside out.

The subject of this poem is purely Death personified. Not so much Death Actual as the poignant awareness, the intimation of mortality and denial of it with which all of us, not just the lovely young girls of Ransom's preoccupation (cf., "Janet Waking," "Here Lies a Lady," "Blue Girls"), defend ourselves as long as we draw breath. In this poem Ransom has invented a dramatic scene, staged on an antebellum piazza, which must be something like a Bread Loaf verandah, and here has placed a young girl moonily awaiting her truelove—a one word catchall for the tryst or rendezvous down the corridors of time. Instead of a stalwart young lover there appears an old gentleman in a dustcoat, and it is the interplay between the two dramatic monologs, the two voices, that carries the freight of the poem. I could cite several other examples of this use of the persona—Browning's "My Last Duchess" is probably one of the best known, or Yeats's Crazy Jane poems.

This brings us to the category I have somewhat awkwardly named the ideational *I*. In these poems, the use of the first-person voice seems to me to be subordinate to establishing the intent of the poem itself, the making of a statement. I immediately think of Robert Frost, who was a great one for unobtrusively carrying out the man-to-nature analogy in a kind of muted, modest, *me* voice. For instance, the well known, perhaps all too often studied poem, "Design," the one that begins: "I found a dimpled spider, fat and white / on a white heal-all holding up a moth / like a white piece of rigid satin cloth . . ." and goes on to make a statement about the dark design that lurks in the apparent innocence of natural laws. Here's the second stanza, and note the absence of the poet's self from it.

What had that flower to do with being white,
The wayside blue and innocent heal-all?
What brought the kindred spider to that height,
Then steered the white moth thither in the night?
What but design of darkness to appall?—
If design govern in a thing so small.

Now Frost wrote from a carefully created pastoral vantage point and he was a sweet deceiver of the mordant comment. By coincidence, this poem too is an Italian sonnet. But I think the first-person voice here serves to introduce a deliberately personal note, partly to bring mankind—human life—into this philosophical orbit, and particularly to anticipate and prepare for the essentially human conclusions of the sestet. A heal-all, to refresh your botanical wisdom, is a wayside weed, and it is usually some shade of purple. This heal-all is diseased. Our usual association to white is to purity, innocence, and virtue. But here the white flower is a dying flower, the white moth is dead and it has been killed by a white spider exercising its natural camouflage. The sestet poses the bitter question: What is the design that underlies this fatal coincidence of whiteness, disease, and death? And at the very end of the poem, Frost makes the suggestion that perhaps there is no design at all, the one possibility more appalling than a deliberate malevolence, the possibility that nothing governs the universe, that all events are an accidental collision. This doctrine of pure chance of course reduces man to the insignificance of a flower or moth on the cosmic scale. But Frost doesn't make a dogmatic statement one way or the other—it is very much his style to suggest, or pose the ambiguity, then, as it were, to walk away from it.

I take as another example W. H. Auden's "September 1, 1939," a poem that was very exciting to me and to my student generation, a poem which begins: "I sit in one of the dives / On Fifty-second Street / Uncertain and afraid / As the clever hopes expire / Of a low dishonest decade." Now this is an ideational poem of the purest kind. It is also one of Auden's most directly didactic poems, the argument developed in direct logical form. The title dates the outbreak of World War II and perhaps parallels Yeats's "September 1913," an elegy for John O'Leary, dead in the cause of Irish independence. The subject is the matter of our common guilt. The poet despairs that our dark unconscious overrules all our conscious, ethical, good intentions. The use of the first person in this poem quite simply makes the dark text palatable, possible, accessible to the reader. Certainly the opening lines help to do that. The despondent poet hunched over his drink in a tavern in Manhattan muses in stanza five on the state of the world:

> Faces along the bar
> Cling to their average day:
> The lights must never go out.
> The music must always play . . .

Auden omitted one stanza from later versions, perhaps because he felt it was self-complacent, or that he had already made his point, or that world events had rendered obsolete his call for the individual to assume responsibility. I quote four of its offending lines:

> . . . no one exists alone;
> Hunger allows no choice
> To the citizen or the police;
> We must love one another or die.

The humanist is speaking here, raising the personal voice of his anguish aloud, the poet who knows full well how futile it is to expect the poet to serve as legislator, acknowledged or unacknowledged. The poet who knows, as he says in the "Elegy for W. B. Yeats," "For poetry makes nothing happen: it survives / In the valley of its saying . . ."

The final pigeonhole I have selected for the first-person voice is the autobiographical poem, for which an ancient and honorable tradition exists. It is an attractive poetry, capable of sustaining a good deal of passion, all the way from Richard Eberhart's "If I could only live at the pitch that is near madness / When everything is as it was in my childhood / Violent, vivid, and of infinite possibility" to Sylvia Plath's anguished cry, "Daddy, you bastard, I'm through." Autobiography is just that, whether it takes the form of poetry or of prose, and it embraces any reminiscence that is particular to the poet. Confessional poems, I think, simply take the process one step further. They are more deeply personal revelations about the poet's psychological struggles, laying him open to censure or sympathy, and can range freely among an investigation of his marital problems, struggle for sanity, sexual identity, losses or occasional triumphs, but more commonly catastrophes. In a sense the confessional poem can be seen as a kind of self-therapy, the poem itself a way of relieving the psychological tension building in the poet. At its best, the confessional poem invites the reader in by enlisting his sympathy and identification. At its best, the specific experiences of the confessional poet embody to some degree the national, or even the international crisis.

Anne Sexton in "The Double Image" opens with a very simple and direct diction, which is, however, quite artfully constructed, relying heavily on end-stopped rhymes.

I am 30 this November.
You are still small, in your fourth year.
We stand watching the yellow leaves go queer,
flapping in the winter rain,
falling flat and washed. And I remember
mostly the three autumns you did not live here.

In this long poem divided into seven sections is compressed a life history: A mother dying of cancer, a nervous breakdown culminating in the removal of a child, and the final though still tentative reconciliation in which the family group is reestablished. The controlling image is that of the two portraits, mother and daughter, being painted during this terrible time, and the further overtone that the small child is herself made in the image of her own mother: "We named you Joy. / I, who was never quite sure / about being a girl, needed another / life, another image to remind me. / And this was my worst guilt; you could not cure / nor soothe it. I made you to find me."

On the whole, I would guess that a bad poem about a brownie or a butterfly will offend poetic tact and taste no less than a bad poem full of self-pitying and clumsily articulated personal details. Critics respond more harshly when their universals are twanged, however; the confessional poem will arouse more choler than the elf or swallowtail. As for categories, frequently they overlap. And in a great poem, the distinction is purely academic.

IV
The Place Where I Live

Journal notes, an essay on raising an orphan foal, the loss of a newborn foal, and a good deal of digressive musing comprise this section. Chronologically constructed, the time frame runs from the summer of 1973 through the late spring of 1978 and spans my transition from weekend and summer visitor to permanent resident in the state of New Hampshire.

Estivating—1973

The reason I am keeping a journal this season of the hearings and the horses is to put down those "bits of the mind's string too short to use," as Joan Didion once said. Things tie themselves together with little quote marks and perhaps the string crosshatches itself into a statement in time, who knows? My son, scanning the *New York Times* one weekday morning when it was heavy with financial articles of the technical sort, complained, "not even anybody good died today" and I hang onto that phrase as it reflects the kind of stasis I am in, estivating here.

I came away from the city the first day of June, no longer in the grip of one routine, promptly though voluntarily snared in another one, for my friend and neighbor across the valley has leased me two mares for the riding and gifted me with two foals for the caring. Some impulse toward order propels me into the nonpermissiveness of animals to care for, a schedule to adhere to. I think I am afraid of too much latitude—how else could I handle such large blocks of time? As it is, I sleep less and more lightly than I have in years. One night the bay

First appeared in *Ploughshares* 2, no. 1 (February 1974).

mare, for reasons of her own, took out a railroad tie and twenty feet of fence board. A week later, the colt and the filly, having spent several hours worrying the top slide board out of its double fixture, exploded out of the barn at 2 A.M. and we went barefoot flapping after them. They wanted only to be in the paddock with the mares, it seems. We want them stabled at night, as they are too young and venturesome to roam. It is a return to the era of earaches and chicken pox and the nightmares of young children. Presumably, it serves some purposes, vague ones: the animal pleasure of touch, an aesthetic gratification, and it uses up some of my maternal obsessions. And is perhaps a way of hanging loose in between some more sustained efforts. Always the small terror of a prolonged block hovering just off stage, waiting to set in like an ice age. In any case, it makes me remember Orwell saying ". . . there has literally been not one day in which I did not feel that I was idling . . . as soon as a book is finished, I begin, actually from the next day, worrying because the next one is not begun and am haunted by the fear that there will never be a next one."

Noondays, I try to think up here in this boxy, pale blue room. I think of Virginia Woolf's aunt who did her the kindness of falling from her horse while riding out to take the air in Bombay and leaving her a legacy for life, enough for that room of one's own. The desk that I sit at in this room is an old oak piece left over from a schoolhouse when the century turned. It has a shallow pencil drawer and two sturdier deep ones and it stands on four unturned legs. Through the window it overlooks an equally unremarkable barn, once a dairy barn for fifty head of Holsteins. In the utilitarian manner of barns it is built into a slope so that one could in all seasons shovel the cow flops downhill and downwind. Years before our tenancy, an artist lived here and favoring the north light for his gloomy canvases—at least the ones he left behind are unremittingly dour in theme and muddy of color—he built an absurd sort of overhang from the haymow. It juts out like a Hapsburg jaw, looming halfway across the one-car-width dirt road that divides house and barn. I can sit here and watch swallows come and go through the gap tooth of an upper board where they coexist with the red squirrels. Yesterday, an owl, late awake in the mizzly weather, flapped his way in, presumably in search of mice. I hope he is snugly tenanted for a while, since he has a habit of hooting his way uphill tree by tree in the small hours announcing something. A very prepossessing paddock connects into the expired dairy farmer's dung heap, now leveled out and used as a shelter for the mares. Except they often prefer to stand out in a downpour, looking woebegone but cool.

From my window I can see the strawberry roan mare tearing up grass by its roots, munching dirt and all, swashbuckling the flies and mosquitoes with her bug repellent-larded tail. Her coloring is rather like that of a redheaded woman, the freckled variety. This, I realize, stands for my four aunts, now deceased, who were always diminishing their spots with cocoa butter.

Privately, I call this mare Amanda and I am writing a cycle of poems for her. She is a sensible and almost never petulant creature, on the enormous side (Aunt Harriet?) with feet as big as dinner plates and the girth of a California wine keg. A broad white blaze down her face lends her a look of continuous startle (Aunt Alma's plucked eyebrows?). And of course that voluptuous golden tail and mane, brillo consistency. She knots these by rubbing on the fence. We spend hours together. I do the combing and she, placidly, enjoys the small sensual tugs of the bristles. Until I was twelve I suffered two heavy plaits of hair, continually coming unbraided. "Stand still!" my mother would say. "Your part is as crooked as Ridge Avenue." Now my mother's hair is as thin and white as spun sugar, coaxed from a baby-pink scalp. This is the kind of reflecting that comes of combing.

Meanwhile, the Watergate unfurls its tattered length daily and we catch bits of it between barn and pond. It is a wondrous decadence, this daytime *opéra bouffe*, beaming in over the hills to this isolated spot. We worm the babies in the middle of John Dean's testimony and at last I see a connection. Although it makes me want to be sick, I count the nematodes in the little ones' shit—forty the first day, fifty-six the next. I am making sure.

Carless, two miles from town, we ride the horses down the back way, through the covered bridge, along the old railroad bed, and come out at the laundromat which was once a station stop on the B & M line. We tie them to the VFW flagpole, fifty yards from the general store. It seems a fitting use. When we remount, milk, flour, butter, and beer in knapsacks, I see that Amanda has left a little pyramid on the lawn.

Mornings, early, we go for long trips over corduroy and dirt roads that have lost their destinations, although the county area map still notes the burying grounds and sugar houses of a hundred years ago. It is chanterelle time, their dry yellow vases nicely visible in the woods at this height. It is like looking for butter. I remember Laurie telling me that in Provence if you want to go mushrooming you must start at daybreak or the other foragers will have picked the woods clean. Here, we can go all day loading our burlap saddle bags with fresh edibles, and not meet another person. It is a delicious depravity, feasting on our find—how far we are from the real world! What does the mushroom know? Only to open the hinges of its gills and shower down its blind spores—white, pink, rusty brown, or the good black of the inky caps. It corrects itself, this fruiting body, it is phototropic. Thanks to gravity, something will fall on fertile ground, though most stay stuck on the gills like words on a page. I suppose I mean that love is like this; as evanescent, as easily lost, as mindless, blind, instinctual. Or it is all a metaphor for the poem, the genesis of the poem as unexpected as the patient mushroom you come upon.

Today I order 200 pounds of horse chow from the Feed and Grain Exchange in the next town. I do this by phone, apologetically, because I have no car and must ask for a delivery. The woman taking my twelve dollar order chats with me, a long and cordial conversation between strangers who will likely never meet. Afterwards, I think about the natural courtesy of it and all the city-surly bank clerks, taxi drivers, and cops who throw this moment into high relief.

Today, two startling finds: an enormous stand of ripe raspberries that fell off their stems into our pails, and yielded twelve jars of jam, and several fresh boletes of a kind I had never seen before. They matched in every way *boletus mirabilis*, which is native to the Pacific Northwest. We ate them gratefully for supper, enfolded into omelets and praised the name and serendipity of their arrival. The mushroom passion freshens with me year by year. Too bad it is such an esoteric subject for Americans—each genus is as distinct as broccoli from cauliflower. A broccoli poem would speak its own universal, but a boletus poem? They are, of course, the toadstools in *Alice* and all those dreadful fairy books of my childhood, each with an elf underneath. Little children are taught to trample them on sight as something nasty to be eradicated. A pity. Once you have eaten wild mushrooms, the dull store-bought agaricus is a poor substitute. I think of Thoreau's "a huckleberry never reaches Boston." I pickle some mushrooms, string others with needle and thread and hang them to dry. Extras I sauté and freeze, but they are a pale imitation of the fresh-picked-and-into-the-pot ones.

This morning I hoed between the corn rows and thought up ways to foil the raccoons who will unerringly arrive with the first ripe ears. A transistor radio tuned to an all-night rock and roll station? Camphor balls and creosoted rope around the perimeter? One of my farmer neighbors claims that balls of newspaper between the rows will keep them off; they dislike the crackle. What to make of the foraging and gathering in? One part thrift, one part madness; three parts inexplicable.

In Yeats's journal, the work sheets for "the fascination of what's difficult" contain these notes: "Repeat the line ending 'difficult' three times, and rhyme on bolt, exult, colt, jolt. One could use the thought of the wild-winged and unbroken colt must drag a cart of stones out of pride because it's difficult." ("I swear before the dawn comes round again / I'll find the stable and pull out the bolt.") But the domestication has got the better of me; lose half a garden and begin again. "Oh masters of life, give me confidence in something." Yeats again. So it seems I put my trust in the natural cycle, and bend to it. It is so far removed from self-improvement as to be an escape hatch. Nature pays me no attention, but announces the autonomy of everything. Here nothing is good or bad, but *is*, in spite of.

Wintering Over

A woman creeps on all fours through a squash patch in mid-September seeking out the late bloomers. The species is called spaghetti squash. Loosely ovoid, pallid green at first, yellowing as it seasons and toughens for winter keeping, it can be boiled, baked, or fried. No matter what culinary approach she takes toward it, the squash concludes as stringy. Seed catalogs have made a virtue of its stubbornly fibrous nature and advertise it as a non-caloric vegetable pasta.

Frost is predicted for tonight. She will cover the tomatoes with an assortment of discarded bed sheets and tablecloths, first setting out pans of water between the plants, for water acts in some perfectly logical scientific way she does not understand to keep the temperature up. It is her annual aim to hold the fruit on the vines until October. Since they live near the top of a hill overlooking the river valley and her tomatoes grow on a south slope along the foundation stones of the house, it is not an unreasonable ambition.

Her son, rattling up the hill in his ten-year-old Dodge,

pronounces that it is time to mow the truck. If he had helped his father more vigorously, the pickup truck would not still hunker on the grassy strip by the barn. The manure in the back, destined last April for the garden located still farther up the hill where the terrain yields a flat and sunny area, has long since put up a fine crop of weeds and grasses. The boy and his father are intermittently repairing the brake line. Each redress on occasional weekends seems to result in another leak farther along the line. The son has lost interest, he is not cause oriented; the young, remarks his father, want instant gratification. He, on the contrary, loves his recalcitrant old truck as fiercely as if it were a runaway.

Her mare is a dangerous runaway. She must recognize this fact of their lives much as one might be forced to acknowledge an alcoholic mother or a retarded child. Therefore of course she does not love her mare the less, but more. She is a rescuer by temperament. Horses one cannot reform are sent, in the country colloquialism, to the canner's. Rather than reduce her mare to dog food, she sends her to be bred. In the third estrus, the mare settles. Gravely and perfectly, the matter is settled, for impending motherhood is said to exert a calming influence on the flightiest mares. Like many folk sayings, it sounds dubious and sexist.

The woods are fecund with mushrooms. Atop the settled mare each morning she rides along familiar trails made surprising by the emergence of parasols and puffballs, hen-of-the-woods, coral, and oysters. Each time she dismounts to pick a treasure the mare sinks her teeth gratefully into a clump of ferns, although ferns are not thought to be a respectable fodder. In this manner they proceed into the hills until the saddlebags are full. Yesterday in the village, casually gracing a lawn and imitating split-seamed baseballs, three brain puffballs appeared. In this week's newspaper, a time-lapsed series of photo-graphs of a giant puffball which had burst the asphalt driveway leading to the Emersons's garage usurped the front page. Coming home she passes a pine log that has lain for years along the dirt road. Today, growing at forty-five-degree angles of inclination, two dog stink-horns. *Phallus impudicus*, the handbook defines them. They are, in outline and dimension, exact Andy Warhol replicas. Is this nature's joke on art? And what of the force that drives the puffball upward against bewildering odds, against the counterforce of gravity reinforced by bitumens pressing down? Mother Seton has just been canonized for curing, among other ills, a documented case of leukemia. Isn't the puffball's defiance of tech-nology a profane miracle?

She goes to an illustrated lecture on the care and management of the brood mare. It is given in the local high school by an apple-cheeked veterinarian who appears to be sixteen years old. Facts strike her as electrons bom-bard the nucleus of the atom. She learns, for example, that there are three criteria for breeding a mare back in the foal heat, the prime one being that the afterbirth weigh at least fourteen pounds and that it separate from the uterus of the mare within two hours of parturition. Colored slides accompany this information. The after-birth, a tattered shawl of membranous blue streaked with red blood and luminous white stripes of tissue, hangs out of the vulva of a bay mare. She is the mother of three children; she has, in her own mother's quaint phrase, been to the well three times. Still, she is startled by a drawing of a uterus full of foal. Diagrams of wrong presentations assault her. Fetuses are portrayed rump first, head first but with front legs drawn back like fish fins, upside down, and sideways wedged. Here, a mare who delivers standing up must be attended, else the foal will fall to the floor and the placenta sever prematurely, draining away one-sixth of the foal's blood supply. She makes a list of items to have in readiness: a Fleet enema, a solution of iodine to swab the umbilical cord (tear, do not cut), a syringe for the tetanus toxoid. She learns more than she had ever wanted to know. The pregnancy is a commitment, from this there is no drawing back. When her mare comes to term this spring she will probably sleep in the barn. She hears the testimonies of others in the class who have spent three, twelve, sixteen nights on army cots outside their gravid mares' stalls. She feels reassured. She is part of a hardy band, a secret cell, an underground of true believers.

When the boy comes up the hill in his red Dodge Dart this September morning it is to see his sister, visiting from Europe where she lives. She is three years his senior and from the time he crept across the kitchen floor to paddle in the dog's water dish and she retrieved him, they have had a mythic bond. Now he is six feet tall, elegantly slender, with the sky-blue eyes of a newborn. A handlebar mustache mutes the fullness of his lower lip while giving his face a gently melancholic, if not world-weary air. He is twenty-two. His sister, although gracefully constructed, is five feet, one inch. So much for genetic similarities.

The mother watches them embrace. Camouflaged, she can afford to conduct some meticulous noticing. They are perfect with their four arms and four legs of mismatched lengths, and their laughter overlaps perfectly. Arms entwined like school children or young lovers, they leave the sun and go indoors. But the afterimage stays, it is as still as ectoplasm, and she can go on seeing them as long as she likes from her dog-squat in the squash patch.

Through two changes of equinox the truck has sustained a flat tire. Not Liquid Wrench nor Naval Jelly nor an entire bottle of Coca-Cola will loosen the rusted lugs. The brake line, the clutch linkage, the little problem with the carburetor have all yielded this day to the double onslaught of father and son. Now they are going to pull the wheel loose with the tractor. Its engine starting up intensifies the chugging of red squirrels who claim overlapping territories in the abandoned apple trees. Nuts rain down unheard from the shagbark hickories and three parasol mushrooms, *lepiota procera*, of seven, nine, and nine-and-one-half-inch diameters, wait to be found in the same bosky dell as last year.

The woman is wearing her farmer pants, bib overalls with cretonne curtain patches where the cloth has worn through. Her son would prefer a mother who dressed in matching beige sweaters and skirts and a single strand of pearls. He would banish yogurt from her refrigerator, horses from her pasture, and yoga from her Tuesday nights. Stress is a physiologic response inappropriate to a situation. Adrenal production rises, muscles bunch in readiness, even the body's coagulation chemistry stands by in case of open wounds. In yoga class on Tuesday nights on a mat in the dank basement of the school that was built in the village ten years after the Civil War, she learns to breathe away stress. She goes through the multiple positions of Sun Worship, she assumes the Cobra, Fish, and Child poses. Her shoulder stands strengthen the lower back and tone up the organs that hang within the abdominal cavity although she is unclear about their relative positions. The instructor's script is banal, relying heavily on images of waves on a beach or clouds in the sky. The beneficial claims made for yoga are possibly ridiculous, she does not believe in astral projection or transcendental processes, but she slips away each week during the meditation period. That is to say, she loses contact. Possibly she dozes off? Whatever it is, it refreshes.

Her son does not like to come upon her practising her shoulder stands. He finds this position ungainly for a woman in middle age. Between mothers and sons the way is slippery. Her lower back aches right now and she slides one hand inside the loose waist of the overalls to massage the sore part, the lifting and bending fulcrum beaten hollow daily by her will. There is still goldenrod at the field's edge. Overhead, an afternoon of calmest blue. The swamp maples are turning already; she thinks of them as cowards. She would hold summer on the stalk another month at least. This was the time of year he traditionally came down with the croup, the little one they wintered over so painfully those early years with the kettle and the smell of tincture of benzoin in the room. His sister braved the steam to play checkers with him, or Fish or Old Maid. They ate fig newtons and the crumbs migrated between the sheets.

Even as the woman suffers these irrefutable nostalgias, three heifers and a young steer with a bald face crash about in the underbrush below the paddock. They have been loose all summer foraging through pockets of lost meadows that the woods enclose and wandering down networks of old logging roads. This mild autumn afternoon, driven perhaps by thirst and a nostalgia for grain, they show themselves. The heifers are Jerseys. At careless first glance they are taken for deer, a prospect that startles. Having survived without human ministrations for several months, all are skittish. Even cornered, soothed with shakes of grain in the bucket, they have a disconcerting way of wheeling abruptly and clattering off into the scrub growth. More than an hour passes before they are penned. The heifers have vaccination tags in their ears. A mile or so clockwise, then counterclockwise about the paddock and the son wrestles one of them still enough so that his sister can call out the number. The veterinarian's wife runs it through her file and locates the appropriate dairy farmer, some fifteen miles distant. He is a man lackadaisical about his fences and his watering trough and unperturbed about his missing animals. Just at nightfall, his barn chores completed, he drives up the hill with his helper in the livestock truck. There was five run off, he insists. Three heifers and two beeves, run off last May, five in all. He does not accuse. Still, his statement sets in motion a new hypothesis after he has safely gone. They could have closeted the steer, at least, in the upper pasture and wintered themselves a good supply of steaks.

In truth, then, one steer has not survived his freedom. The woman sees him down somewhere in deep woods, trapped in a tangle of old barbed wire or fallen into an abandoned well. The others rush off, cattle fashion, from danger. She has a vision of that slow death. Indeed, she will come upon the skeleton one year hence, still wearing tags of its hide and pearl chips of cartilage. It is stretched on its side as if it had died in its sleep. Her horse will shy harshly from the mound that says mildly on the air, carrion.

They make a late supper after the excitement. The air has sharpened since sunset. An almost-full moon slips up over the next hill. Both wood stoves are going, popping their cheeks from time to time. Outdoors, the tomato plants under their old bed sheets have taken on the outlines of white dinosaurs. It is all in vain. Nothing green can be had in trade this night. The horses sleep standing up, silently growing their winter coats as a hard frost rides in leaving a trail of white prints on the grass, the rooftop, the forgotten handbook of mushrooms left open to dog stinkhorn.

Bringing up Boomerang

Some of my writer friends traveled in Europe last summer. One holed up in Nantucket and completed a draft of a novel. Several served on the staffs of writers' conferences. I spent three months in rural New Hampshire ministering to an orphan foal.

How does a human get so involved with horses that she can spend hours every day in their large and redolent company?

It goes like this. When I was a small child growing up in Philadelphia's then-fashionable suburb of Germantown, the garbage wagons were still drawn by horses. So were most of the milk wagons. One winter I gave away my three older brothers' camp blankets to various forlorn-looking draft horses as they toiled up our hill.

It wasn't as if there had been no animals in my life; on the contrary, we were a family that "had" dogs. A succession of them ran away or were struck by cars or were poisoned by phobic neighbors. It seemed we were always beginning again with a puppy, which was never allowed abovestairs and each night was incarcerated in the cavernous cellar. When the poor beast howled at night, I frequently snuck down into the gloom and curled up with it on the discarded shag rug allotted for its bed. The cellar was warm and the rug was a thick one, but my deed was more heroic than it sounds. I was terrified of the dark, but even more terrified that turning on a light would alert my parents. In those days, sensible children reserved their most extreme fear for the wrath of the elders.

Cats were forbidden; my mother never trusted cats. They were known to leap into baby carriages and suck away the infant's breath. I confess I never developed anything deeper than respect for cats. They are good mousers who keep the barn free of vermin.

Horses, surprisingly, *were* considered respectable creatures. I was permitted to take weekly riding lessons at a nearby livery stable, but punished for staying late to groom and feed and shovel manure. In truth, as the youngest of four children I felt an empathy with the animal world that was not manifest in the human one. I was wanted. I was doing a job. Moreover, manure mixed with wood shavings smelled better to me than perfume. At the risk of coprophilia, I confess it still does.

Shall we now take into account Sigmund Freud and the Horse as Phallus? The young girl's interest in horses, according to the Master, is the socially acceptable sublimation of her sex drive. Horses symbolize dominance. Girls love the feeling of being in control of, and astride, all that power. When boys come cantering into the normal girl's life, horses back out of it. By implication, those females who experience no diminution of interest in horses after the onset of puberty are locked in internal struggle, ripe for neuroses, and will in time provide a rich pasture for the expensive romp of the psychoanalyst.

I deny nothing. I attend all hypotheses *qua* hypotheses. Freud's theories of female sexuality have now been substantially discredited, if not debunked. But the pathology of my own case is clearly linked to those dark-green, all-wool camp blankets with their embroidered S for Camp Shoshonee that rode down Carpenter Lane one by one on the bony rumps of the garbage collectors' jades. All my childhood I was a closet "Keeper of the Beasts." It seems I am still collecting and blanketing—rugging, it's called—the castoffs.

The story of Boomerang, my orphan foal, begins with such a rescue mission. Two years ago, for the price she was to fetch from the slaughterer, I bought a sad-eyed, gravely undernourished mare. Taboo was a topography of saddle sores. Her tongue had been torn nearly in two with a wire bit. Her vertebrae and hipbones were vividly enough defined to provide an anatomy lesson for a zool-ogy class. Her owner, operating on the theory that the less you feed a spirited horse the slower it will go, had been starving her, to no avail; she had run off with her last three riders.

Taboo was gradually restored to normal horse silhou-ette. I exercised her on the longe line at first; the horse describes a circle around the trainer and learns to walk, trot, and canter on voice command. Then I rode her, timorously, while a friend worked the longe line. Finally, unattached, I began to walk and trot her in the ring. She was wonderfully smooth and responsive.

That spring, when I went trail-riding for the first time with a friend, Taboo clamped down on the bit and ran away with me for two miles. We raced her mythological wolves at a flat-out gallop down a hard-packed dirt road at high noon. The wind rushed in my mouth and took away my breath. Dying will be like this, I thought. Dying will happen around the next bend. Luckily, I met no

one coming the other way, although I remember glimps-
ing a very surprised fisherman as we clattered over a
wooden bridge and flew inexorably onward.

Having survived that forty-mile-an-hour ordeal, I
learned to ride alone, and to canter only on the steepest
hills so I could somewhat control this schizophrenic
mare.

Why don't you breed her? my horse friends all sug-
gested as the season turned. Mares have a way of settling
down after they're bred. You'll see how calm and docile
she'll be after she's had a foal.

Taboo came unmistakably and definitively into heat
on June 30. She squealed and squirted urine and rubbed
her tail on the barn side until the top hairs fell out. Awaj,
the local Arabian stallion, serviced her on each of four
successive mornings. Forty-nine days later, she caught
me in an inattentive moment and ran away with me
again. Once I had her in hand, I walked home, shaken. It
was no use. She would have to go to the knacker. Death
and dog food awaited this beautiful crazy horse. Then,
just like a television soap, the vet called with news of
the blood test. Taboo had "settled"; Awaj had gotten
her pregnant.

And she did settle down as the pregnancy progressed.
During the last two months of that eleven-month-long
gestation, I rode her bareback so as to spare her the dis-
comfort of the girth around her swollen barrel. It was
blackfly time; I wore a beekeeper's hat to defend against
them. She wore her gauze ear-bonnet, which ties under
the throat, for the same purpose. Since she was shoeless,
I put on the winter Easyboots, weird but effective con-
traptions of polyurethane that are custom-designed for
each hoof. Even so, they have a way of coming loose in
snow, and since they are notoriously hard to locate,

white on white, I had painted them red. Thus sallied forth the eccentric woman and her strangely gotten-up horse with its red toenails!

On the night of June 2, Taboo foaled. The little buckskin filly was on her feet whinnying in a moment. And then the nightmare began. The mare, snorting with panic in a far corner of the stall, would not allow the newborn to approach her. Each time it nosed blindly against her flanks, hungry to suck, she bit and kicked it.

A frantic call to the vet at 1 A.M. Never had I felt guiltier, not even when I awakened the pediatrician for advice about earache. Twitch the mare and back her into a corner every two hours, was the vet's advice. If the foal doesn't get the colostrum—the first milk secreted by the mammary glands immediately after birth—it won't get the antibodies necessary for its survival. A twitch, for the uninitiate, is a metal pincers or loop of rope used to restrain a horse by tightening it around the animal's upper lip. Even subdued with a twitch and with her hindquarters backed into a corner of the stall where she could do the least damage kicking, Taboo was a terror. The pathetic little battered foal went on fighting for her birthright, getting ten or twelve hungry sucks at a time.

We went through this medieval torture every two hours around the clock for the first day, every four hours thereafter. On the morning of the third day we separated the two forever. Taboo the unwilling mother, turned out to pasture, recovered rapidly. Boomerang the foal, imprinted from the first on the intervening humans who had saved her life, regards people still as her mother-surrogates. We bottle-fed her for about four days and then were able to wean her to a pail. This is easier than it sounds; horses drink by sucking rather than lapping. The amazing thing was how rapidly thirty-two ounces of formula went down. Because Boomerang's forelegs were too long and her neck too short to drink from a pail set on the ground—after all, nature had designed her to suckle standing up—we built a little stand on pegs to hold the bowl of milk. A few weeks later, we did the same with a grain box.

It was hard not to hate the rejecting mare. It was even harder to put up with the jocularity about women's lib that she and I were subject to. For half the town turned out to ogle at the miracle of the orphan foal who had not only survived her ordeal but showed every sign of growing up to be a well-made pedigreed filly. I developed a certain paranoia. How many minutes into the conversation would it take for each man who sauntered up the hill to say something terribly clever and snide about the role of the female?

Nodding his head at the mare grazing in an adjoining pasture, my farrier said, "Guess she's been readin' *Ms* magazine" (one minute).

The vet, an affable, unflappable man, bending over to stitch the foal's worst cut, offered, "You shouldn't've given her all those books on bein' modern" (two minutes, thirty seconds).

"That's a damn smart mare," the man who raises vealers said. "Why'n't you get her some trousers and she can go to the city?" (20 seconds).

I remembered the look of terror in the mare's eyes, how she quivered and trembled when the foal struggled out of the amniotic sac, rocked and swayed finding its balance, and staggered toward her. She seemed to say, "What happened? I had a little cramp and lay down for a minute and when I got up there was a ghost in the stall!"

I remembered my own terror in childbirth-before-the-Enlightenment: how alien that screaming bundle of raw flesh seemed, wrapped in white cloth and presented to my awkward arms!

I remembered how excruciating the nursing process had been. My nipples cracked and bled afresh with every session. After five days of agony every four hours, I capitulated. The hungry baby made a happy transition to bottled formula. I came down with what was then called "milk fever" and suffered the conclusion that I was not made for suckling my young. That deprived infant and the two who followed were raised on cow's milk and Karo syrup diluted with water and boiled to a fare-thee-well.

And I remembered the hiss of discomfort, that sharp intake of breath on the mare's part every time the foal nuzzled its way to her milk bag. When the little one finally clamped onto a teat, the mare was almost unrestrainable. Pain, I thought, unmitigated by maternal instinct or social pressure. Sigmund, where are you now when I need you? I was relating all over the place.

It is not unflattering to be followed about by a foal. The general public does not realize that you represent MILK. The general public cherishes a fantasy of loyalty, love, and little-lamb enduring values. That filly would have left me in an instant for a welcoming mare with milk in her bag. As it was, she had to make do with Borden's Foal-lac, a milk replacer supplemented with every known vitamin and trace mineral and almost as expensive, ounce for ounce, as good Scotch whisky. The twenty-five-pound cans (at thirty-three dollars a can) come impishly illustrated with a photograph of a cow wearing a saddle and bridle, an anomaly I came to loathe at two in the morning as I mashed and stirred the lumpy formula into a potable gruel. Since our other horses are turned out all night in summer, at least I did not have to contend with a barnful of inquisitive geldings when I went down with the copper bowl from an old chafing dish which exactly fitted the stand we had built.

May it be said in Borden's favor that they also manufacture Foal-lac in pellet form. By the end of the first month, Boomer had acquired four teeth and a certain hazy notion of the texture of solids. She spilled as many as she chewed, but came to love a mixture of regular grain and the magic expensive pellets. We kept her on her early morning "fix" of warm formula, however, long after the other milk feedings had been gradually and sneakily withdrawn. The first morning I arrived in her stall with pellets and grain only, she knocked me flat in her ten-week-old zeal to discover where the hot milk was hiding.

Even so, in a way it was less traumatic than the normal weaning. All too often, mare and foal shriek piteously to each other for days after separation. And then, just when your sanity has eroded to the hardpan madness that lurks beneath all our frontal lobes, they lose interest in each other. Two weeks after that, they have forgotten the maternal-filial relationship altogether. They are, miraculously, strangers and may now become friends. . . . Not without its appeal, that notion, to us mothers for life.

What a mare teaches her foal are the normal precautionary measures even a domestic beast must take: flee the unusual sound or movement; be wary of strangers; come when called, and above all, emulate me. On the first day of Boomer's life a septic tank was being installed, an operation that involved a backhoe and a bulldozer not fifty feet from her stall. Carpentry, meanwhile, was proceeding overhead to the tune of an air compressor that seats the started nails and stutters like a machine gun. With that for normal background noise, there is little indeed that spooks this filly. As for caution regarding strangers, people in her orphan brain are safe and warm and food providing. Thus she has accepted the halter and lead shank almost without question. She stands to have her feet lifted one by one and tapped on in preparation for the age when she will be shod. Come when called, yes, and answer with a whinny. She greets me at feeding time with a basso little nicker. As for emulation, the situation is fuzzy. Instinct has prevailed; she has learned to graze. She bucks and rears and races for the hell of it, dodging about as nimbly as a goat, and when she runs at her happiest, she carries her tail straight up, like a deer's scut.

Today, Boomerang is five months old and growing fast. The trees are leafless now. There is a cutting edge to the north wind. Nature has responded by providing her with a fuzzy winter coat, far thicker than the coats adult horses develop each autumn. I've just spent an hour repairing a stretch of fence that had yielded to some large-scale leanings and scratchings. As I head back down the pasture toward the barn, Boomer whinnies shrilly. She is torn between staying in the field with the other horses and following me to the paddock. I don't turn back. She hesitates, then, just before I drop out of her line of vision, comes racing after me. I stay for a few minutes in the paddock, tousling her much as you might tousle a large dog. She nuzzles and nudges me for more. As with an affectionate dog, more is never enough. After I duck through the fence and head toward the house, she stands for a few minutes at the rail to make sure I mean it. Finally, she trots back out to the upper field, rejoining the geldings and the mare.

She has taken up a lot of slack in my life, that one. Between teaching commitments and my own writing, to say nothing of the daily exigencies of a country life in which we grow our own vegetables and cut our own wood, it is a life not noted for slack to begin with. But living in and with the world of the physical is a release from the world of the mind. Paradoxically, I find mucking out stalls each morning a fine and private time for thinking. The poet in me is fed. I am deeply nurtured, I think, by the animals I deal with and observe, from the chipmunk that lurks under Boomer's feedbox or the fox that enters the paddock at night to sit and bark, to the horses themselves, those immense presences. "Animals are honest through their inability to lie," I said in a poem. Their instinctual responses, their lack of guile, their physical grace, and their intellectual limitations all move and work in me.

And of all animals, surely a foal is the chief aesthetic delight. Sometimes, leaving Taboo out of it, I think how much I'd like another one. Anybody out there with a proven brood mare in need of a kind home?

Journal—Late Winter-Spring, 1978

13 February 1978 Today, in the dying butternut tree that holds up the clothesline from which depend various suets and the main sunflower-seed feeder, an owl. Peterson's indicates it is a barred owl, not an unusual bird in these surroundings. He arrived, like a poem, unannounced. He squatted on the branch, puffed to an almost perfect roundness against the cold. His gray and brown and buff markings imitate the landscape of tree branch and caterpillar nest tatters against the snow. I could not, as the cliché has it, believe my eyes at first, and tried to make him into some recognizable artifact of nature—a clump of windblown leaves, for example. Like the notes for a poem, he would not go away but merely swelled there passively all through breakfast.

The squirrels did not show themselves, wisely. The chickadees are fearless, or at least know they have nothing to fear. The blue jays likewise. I note that our narrow-faced, downside-traveling nuthatches were absent all day.

14 February The owl is a Cheshire cat of an owl, noiselessly appearing, disappearing, flapping off soundlessly

---

on immense wings, returning, higher up than before. He swivels his head almost 360 degrees, like a Japanese puppet-balloon held aloft on a stick. The face is infinitely old, infinitely wise, very catlike. Perched, no wings or claws are evident, lending him even more mystery than is warranted. Like the finished poem, he makes it all seem easy. Not since last winter's wild turkeys, not since last summer's swallow nestling sideshow on the front porch stringers has there been better indoor viewing.

15 February This resident owl of ours, I muse on the third day of his tenure in the butternut, resembles nothing birdlike. Most of all he looks like a baseball pitcher in a tight spot, winding up, swiveling to check the runners at first and second, then . . . the balk. The old owls of my poems were of the furtive sort, night hooters. Whenever I did catch a daytime glimpse of them, they were in a hurry to get under cover and they seemed ragged, weary, diminished by a hard night's work. This one is larger than life-size. He has assumed the stature of a godhead in the birdfeeding zone, though today he and the squirrel eyed each other and nothing happened. Perhaps the owl is full of his nightly mice? I noticed that the squirrel took care, while cleaning up the spilled sunflower husks, not to turn his back on the owl. Although only a small red squirrel, perhaps he is too large to tempt even an enlarged owl.

20 February The filly these cold mornings canters in place in her stall. Too excited to tuck into her morning hay, she wants desperately to be let out, to run off some of that adolescent exuberance. Some days it is impossible to get a halter on her before her morning run. Today I unleashed her early and stood in the barn doorway to enjoy the aesthetics of her romp. The young horse is so improbably gracefully made; the body itself has not yet filled out, the legs are still disproportionately long. That extraordinarily high tail carriage, the whole plume of it arched over her back, and the floating suspended gait she displays at the trot are inherited from her pure Arabian sire. It takes quite a lot of racing, dodging, cavorting, and bucking to get the morning kinks out. She can come to a dead stop from, say, thirty miles an hour. She can attain that speed in, say, three strides. What she does is harsher than ballet, and less controlled, something like dribbling down a basketball court, feinting, shooting, wheeling, back to the other end, and so on. The exultation I feel as I watch her move so freely and with such exhilaration is a kind of glorying in effortlessness, no matter how much muscle is involved. She moves the way a poem ought to move, once it's crafted.

24 February Putting in the spiles I lean on the brace and bit, having to use all my weight to keep the metal spiral angling upward into the tough tree. How astonishing, after the hole is bored, that the sap glistens, quivers, begins to run freely. To think that I have never seen or done this before! I am as captivated as the city child finding out where milk comes from.

We have cobbled a Rube Goldberg sort of contraption for boiling the sap down: an ancient kitchen sink for an evaporator, leftover bits of corrugated metal roofing to enclose the fire, a rack and grill from a long-abandoned fireplace gadget that was designed to throw heat back into the room but failed to do so to an appreciable degree, and two rusty pieces of stovepipe, one with a damper. Plus piles of trash wood, pine, primarily, which gives off too much pitch to be safe to burn indoors.

1 March Although it is still too cold for any appreciable melt, one tree—we note that it's on higher ground than the others and thicker, too—is really running. The sap freezes almost as much as it drips, forming a great color-less cake of possibility. John Burroughs, quoted by the Nearings in their maple syrup text, says: "The first run, like first love, is always the best, always the fullest, al-ways the sweetest."

How much still is dormant! And how the spirit yam-mers at the spirit hole, howling for spring to inch in. Now the horses are shedding, a gradual, indifferent sort of daily loss. Both Jack and the Boomer have grown an extra outer coat of coarse, short white guard hairs. These fly off in the slightest wind or are rubbed off, with grunts of horse pleasure, as they roll in the sun on the snow. Truffle, a mare of more refinement and considerable blood lines, pure bay, has no such tough outer layer. Now that she is eight months pregnant she rolls only on one side, gets up, lies down anew to roll onto the other. Three months still to go. The foal will come at the end of May, in the full throat of spring.

Today I started half a dozen flats for the garden, of French celery and big-leaved basil, broccoli and cauli-flower, and, optimistically because they always die of indoor wilt before it is time to set them out, some min-iature hybrid tomatoes. Our bedroom is now crowded with trays hogging the available south light of two win-dows. Step stools, their step sides facing the windows, make ideal shelves on top of the counter that runs along the south wall. The secret is that I put some aged manure in the bottom of each tray. I hope it is sufficiently an-cient so that it won't, at room temperature, begin to reek.

7 *March* The chickadees have changed their tune and are now singing their mating song. Those same beggars who perched on my arm in January while I was filling

their feeder now stay away most of the morning. They are citizens of independent means.

11 March Everything is softening. The change, when it came, was direct, happened overnight. In spite of longing, reaching for it for weeks, we were still overtaken. The sap is running, a delightful chorus of plink-plinks in the sugarbush. The horses are shedding apace. They itch enough to roll every morning now, all the guard hairs a drift of fuzz in the air, free to nesting birds for the taking.

The other night we did the barn chores together and stood a while enjoying Jack enjoying his hay. Wise old campaigner, he totes it by the mouthful to his water bucket and dunks as he crunches, not unlike the way our forebears crunched sugar lumps as they sucked up their tea. Soon the surface of Jack's water is a yellowish froth from the hayseeds. Alternately he sucks and chews, a moist rhythm.

13 March The morning one is convinced it is spring there is a rising, manic elation for having outlasted the winter, for having come through, in Conrad's phrase, unscathed, with no bones broken. Last evening at feeding time two crows went across the paddock cawing in midair, and I felt goosebumps rising at the nape of my neck. That crows know when to return! That ice will melt, snow cover shrink, days lengthen! Nothing is to be taken for granted after a winter of 20-below-zero mornings, ice frozen in all the water buckets, the horses' nostrils rimmed with ice. After north winds that scour and cleanse and punish. After nights so cold the house clapboards crack and whine. Now the bad times ebb. The split wood lasted, we shall even have a cord or so to spare, as a hedge toward next winter. We calculated correctly on the hay, we congratulate ourselves on its quality, none of it

184

dusty or moldy, enough of it so we can be generous. And Truffle now swelling and swelling, retreating more into herself, less sociable, more self-protective. In a few more weeks we will separate her, almost nine months of her eleven-month gestation now over.

15 March Of mud, muck, and mire. Of the first, the *American Heritage Dictionary* says: "wet, sticky soft earth." Mire is deep, slimy soil or mud whereas muck is (1) "a moist, sticky mixture, especially of mud and filth," or, (2) "moist animal dung mixed with decayed matter and used as a fertilizer." Ergo, manure. Then there's to muck about, British, a synonym for puttering. To muck up is to mismanage, and the usage most common in these parts, to muck out, synonymous with to redd up, make tidy or clean, to put in order, usually before company comes, probably, says the *American Heritage* again, from ridden, to rid. Of mud, muck, and mire: they epitomize the general condition of the paddock at this season of steady, inexorable melt while our whole small world runs downhill, everything a rivulet.

The purest variety of mud squelches upward from the bases of the maple trees from which it is now necessary to gather sap twice a day. I carry ten gallons uphill twice a day. Mucking out, I displace and wheel off two barrow-loads at a cleaning, I estimate forty pounds worth. This does not count wielding the ice chopper each morning to free the sliding barn doors which are kept shut to discourage further inflowing of melt. What we want is outflow. We chip channels through the frozen barn floor, a tundra of semipermafrost, sawdust bedding, hay sprinklings, and manure, and build a dam across the inside lip to coax and cajole a downward, outward flow of what must necessarily all turn to water by May.

Life is hard, it says between my shoulderblades.

Every day the sap gets hauled uphill from twenty taps to metal trash barrels set in the snow at a point where the land thinks better of it and levels off for a respite. The pioneers called these flat places kiss-me-quicks, little plateaus where they could halt the team for a breather. We boiled in our contraption for two windy days. It is sooty, cold, discouraging work, stoking and restoking the fire. At the end of each day we ladled the remaining four gallons into the canning kettle and set it indoors on the Jøtul overnight. Next morning I finished the syrup on the gas stove; it surpasses the fanciest grade triple-A boughten variety. Ours is even paler, purer, and has a buttery taste to it. We are full of grimy complacence. But what a lot of work! By rights maple syrup ought to cost five hundred dollars a gallon. Anything less is a swindle.

22 March Statistics acquired at Saturday's all-day brood-mare clinic run by the University of New Hampshire's extension service. The room was full of a hundred horse-proud people much like me. "Each stallion is a person," proclaimed the stud manager of Vermont's one Thoroughbred breeding farm. "The egg of the mare is about the size of a grain of sand, or one-two hundredth of an inch." She is born with approximately fifty thousand of them. A stallion will produce from seven to ten billion sperm per day. Five hundred million are sufficient for good fertilization. Exhaustion trials indicate that five or six mares per day are optimal, even for a young stud. The sperm is one-two thousandth of an inch in length. We saw many swimming about in slides projected on the screen.

"A mare," says the old-timey polo-playing vet, Stephen Roberts, "a mare is like a Vermonter: an animal that thinks otherwise."

A foal comes out into the air like a diver entering the water, in that position, front hooves on either side of cheek bones. The mare in labor can exert 170 pounds per square inch of pressure, so rotate a wrongly placed foal between contractions, otherwise you may get your arm broken. A lactating mare will yield up to fifty pounds of milk per day. The incidence of twinning is extremely rare, less than 1 percent of live births. Although twinning occurs in 15 to 20 percent of conceptions, these almost invariably abort before the eighth month. Safe, viable births are rare with twins, mostly because the mare is not constructed to house two fetuses. One ends up taking up most of the placental area. Even if she delivers two, she "hasn't the mentality," says Roberts, to take care of two and must be separated from them except at feeding time, for fear she'll step on one, sleep on one, forget one, and so on. Something new to worry about.

6 April Of the Clivus Multrum and fruit flies, this note. The owners of Clivi Multra are not unlike Mercedes owners, which is to say, obsessed with the special nature of their possession. My cousin by marriage, the Mercedes owner, feels for his car the same affection I feel for my animals. He respects, even honors his machine's idiosyncrasies. The keeper of the Clivus Multrum displays the same sort of bemused pride, but with more justification. These earth toilets, waterless, self-composting aerobic indoor privies, are the wave of the future, even though one New Hampshire town has vetoed the installation of any within its jurisdiction. Unquestionably, it is a better arrangement. Can one adjust after all these years of rigorous bathroom hygiene, years of the sound of the redemptive flush carrying off our wastes and gallons of precious water, to the silent slanting cavern of fiberglass? I am uneasy squatting there. Our friends' Clivus, an hour north of us in true sugarbush country, has been in operation over a year now. They claim, indeed boast of success with it. Then over martinis they confess, as the Mercedes cousin might to an unidentifiable squeak, confess to an infestation in the Clivus of fruit flies.

I have sent away this day for a five-month supply of stingless hymenoptera, small, bite-free wasps that prey on the larvae of most of our common flies, stable flies, face flies, house flies, and so on. Fruit flies are also mentioned in the prospectus. One sprinkles the monthly shipment upon the manure pile or on fresh manure in the pasture (or down the Clivus, I should think) and Nature, urged on a little, does the rest.

28 April No peepers yet. The trees are still bare though the lilacs are budding. Daffodils in bloom yesterday, willow showing yellow shoots, forsythia still without color. Such a slow season! Or is it the annual impatience? Nothing much above ground in the pastures, but the horses are full of vinegar so they must be getting some vitamins from the browse.

Coming back home from a week in Salt Lake City where spring abounded, skies were blue and weather balmy is, contrary to expectation, not a downer. It's the secret knowledge that I'm to have two springs that buoys me. It's enough to make one accept the Resurrection in all its dogmatic regalia. If ferns can, if the wake robin trillium can, if the coprinus mushroom on the manure pile can flourish so showily, then He is risen.

Our visiting mare, Shandy Dancer, all sixteen-and-a-half dapple gray Thoroughbred hands of her, arrived last Wednesday in the rain. Much confusion and outrage at first. Gentle Truffle took considerable umbrage at being turned out with this stranger and would at first not allow the new mare closer than a strong stone's throw. Boomerang, unused to strangers, responded in two ways.

First, she made her jaw-clacking, lips-pulled-back submission gesture, the one that says, I am but a suckling foal, do not harm me. Then, perplexed as to gender and in the throes of her first heat, she flagged (raised her tail) and squirted urine. Jackanapes, king that he is, although gelded, strutted, bucked, shook his mighty neck, and tossed his head. The fence between the two sections of pasture, much of it my own handiwork, has given way in a few places. The rails are hemlock, the posts range from twelve to fourteen feet apart, and the span is too great to take the strain of all the rubbernecking going on between two sets of horses. Every morning I go out with my galvanized nails, hammer, and some short pieces of hemlock for mending. It's now a pretty patchy, poor-mouth sort of fence, but it's holding.

This morning we were remembering when Jack first came to live with us and how he cowered, far from Elephant Child's hooves, meekly holding back till last by many lengths when the crew filed in for supper, or out of a morning. He knew his place in the pecking order. Now he is President for Life, a real banana republic-style dictator, and he keeps all the others in line. Oddly, he never kicks or nips Boomer. When he wants her to move on he pushes her forward with his lowered head, like a great hornless ox.

29 April This last week of April, all those little lurchings toward spring have landed us smack in the middle of the season. Pine siskins, crossbills, evening grosbeaks are back. Robins, redwing blackbirds, and cowbirds are back. The indefatigable barn swallows are back, swooping and diving hard for the first insects. My flats of tomatoes are now hardening out on the porch; they look healthy enough to flourish in the earth in a few more weeks. The broccoli and cauliflower have been transplanted into the cold frame where they seem to be standing still, sulking. All my winter dill died while I was in Utah. But the parsley we kept as a house pet right through from October is bushy and strong and as of today is back out of doors. Early peas are going in today.

Some few blackflies are abroad, particularly in the pasture when the wind dies. Just enough to remind us of the incursion to come. Just enough to make me want to press on with planting before they peak.

15 May Who can keep a journal past the first week of May? All in a one-day seizure, cattails, fiddlehead ferns, and nettles up for the foraging. Nettle soup for supper. Three days later, marsh marigolds, which my neighbor Henry calls, as the British do, cowslips. The exquisite tedium of preparing the garden, plowing in last winter's manure, adding lime, destoning, smoothing with the patience if not the dexterity of frosting a cake. If you live with an engineer, you respectfully measure and line up your rows, keep a garden plan on graph paper and do your homework. Did I add half a day's labor to refurbish the fence of chicken wire, eight inches of which is buried to foil woodchucks, moles, voles, and mice? Meanwhile the air has filled with blackflies. Some days, if we dare to speak out of doors, we inhale them. Some days, like this one, a blessed breeze holds them hovering at bay.

May means grass, manna to the horses after a winter on hay. They set about browsing with ferocious intensity. The tonic of spring juices creates a considerable amount of whinnying and squealing and racing, ruckus of the variety called horsing around. Everyone has lost his/her winter coat. The filly positively shines, like a simonized Jaguar. Truffle is ponderous and grave, she walks as though her feet hurt and perhaps they do, as she totes that heavy unborn foal from day to day.

Fulsome bird life. The feeder overcrowded with yellow warblers, rose-breasted grosbeaks, purple finches, and half a dozen goldfinches queued up on the clothesline awaiting an opportunity. The swallows are nesting. They made their usual slapdash repairs to the nests over the brick terrace and once the eggs are hatched will shriek alarm and dive-bomb me if I dare to exit through that door. My peas are up, tentatively. The onions seem off to a strong start.

The peepers were later this year than any year I can remember. They did not give voice until May 8 and only this week have they found their true range. Once they're in full swing, it is deafening to walk by the lower pond at sunset. It is the purest form of noise pollution.

19 June   I could not write this before today. It is three weeks since the morning I found Truffle's stillborn foal sprawled on its side in her stall, and Truffle lying quietly beside it, the placenta still trailing from her vagina. She had delivered it only moments before, a big, possibly too big, seal brown filly, still warm to my touch, one eye glinting as if with life, the mouth slightly ajar so that its pink tongue, brilliantly pink in the graying 5 A.M. light, shone with the promise of life.

The vet came an hour later. He could find no cause but insisted it had never breathed. It had died either before or during its trip to the outside. I am not yet through blaming myself for not being there during Truffle's labor. She had shown no sign, no colostrum waxing on her teats, no restlessness the night before when at 10 P.M. I made my final check of the barn. I remember that I felt her milk bag (for the hundredth time), felt her belly, and gave her a bit more hay. I go back and replay that day before, that evening before, I even replay the early dawn when I think now I heard a kick in the barn, a knock that might have been the portent. Had I dressed and gone to her stall then, had I waked fully and hurried out at that signal, we might have a healthy foal on the ground. These are the things I chew on, worrying them like the smooth gum space of an absent tooth.

We dug a grave behind the old chicken coop, dug and pickaxed and crowbarred away the stones, scooped and shoveled in a drench of early-morning, avid mosquitoes. Then we lifted the lovely heavy corpse into the wheelbarrow. The head lolled, hanging out, and I then cradled it and eased it back behind the rim of the barrow. I especially remember the little protective fuzz hairs that lined the ears, it was as perfectly made as that. We laid the foal in the earth and I got down beside it and folded the long legs in, tucking them back into fetal position, and then we shoveled the earth back over it and finally packed the top with stones so that nothing would disturb the grave.

It is already green there now.

A horse-friend from New York state writes me her condolences. She too has lost not one foal, but twin Thoroughbreds. "I would have spared you this shared experience if I could," she says. According to some astrological prognosticatory chart, we are both sixes on the scale. Sixes, Mary Beth writes, practice all their lives to die well, "act as Morticians of All Life and hold private burying rituals in their hearts."

So it is. So it has been. Truffle, two days later, was quite herself again. Her milk never came in, so she was spared the discomfort of a swollen udder. She never grieved. She licked the dead foal when I came into her stall that morning. She nudged it once or twice with her muzzle, and when it did not respond, simply turned away.

O to turn away.